LUTHERAN

ST. MATTHEW
Stony Plain, Alberta

"Hundred Years Completed"

A Sequel
1985 - 1994

VOLUME 2

ISBN: 978-1-990265-07-5

Hundred Years Completed - A Sequel - Volume 2
St. Matthew Lutheran Church

First Edition: May 1995
Second Edition: June 2021

Additional Copies may be purchased from: W.C.H.F.
#374-9768-170 Street
Edmonton, Alberta
CANADA, T5T 5L4

Typeset and Printed by Heritage Books - Canada #374, 9768-170 Street Edmonton, Alberta
Canada, T5T 5L4

Acknowledgements

St. Matthew Lutheran Church and Congregation of Stony Plain, Alberta wish to recognize and gratefully acknowledged the following persons and organizations for their direct and specific contributions in the publication of this one hundredth anniversary book. May this publication be henceforth a continuous reminder of our founding families and pastors who through faith and prayers and with God's Divine help have forged for us today a church structure and congregation which shall for all time stand as the symbol of hope and the sanctuary of peace.

1. Families and individuals who supplied pictures, photographs, documents and research information.

2. Individuals who did the proof reading and supplied individual reports.

3. Concordia Publishing House, St. Louis, Missouri, USA archival resource.

4. Jack C. Schram provided translations from German to English.

5. Lutheran Historical Institute, Edmonton, Alberta, Canada archival resource.

6. Zion Evangelical Lutheran Church, Snohomish, Washington, USA archival resource.

7. "The Stony Plain Reporter", Stony Plain, Alberta archival resource and anniversary promotion.

8. "The Examiner", Spruce Grove, Alberta anniversary promotion.

9. Roland Hennig and Eric Baron archivists of researched material and historic photographs and documents for St. Matthew history publication.

10. Reuben A. Bauer, commissioned by St. Matthew Lutheran Church as the official printer, publisher, editorial consultant and coordinator for the entire book publication project.

11. Funding for this publication provided for by Eric J. Baron.

"We *Preach Christ*
and Him Crucified"

The Two Volumes

"Ninety Year History"

"Hundred Years Completed"

are

Dedicated to the

Memory of the Pioneers and Founders

of St. Matthew Evangelical Lutheran Church

(Lutheran Church - Canada)

Stony Plain, Alberta

Canada

Table of Contents

Part One Historical Flashbacks and Reminiscing

Part Three Confirmation ... **"something steadfast and sure"**

Part Four Cemetery ... **"departed saints recognized"**

Part Five A Century **of Service, Commitment and Praise**

Part One

Historical   Flashbacks
and
Reminiscing .

This photograph is the earliest known record of St. Matthew Lutheran Church of Stony Plain, Alberta. The church, with parsonage at one end, was constructed in 1894 and dedicated in late summer of that year. Rev. and Mrs. Eberhardt can be seen to the left of the picture.

Founders of St Matthew Lutheran Church, Stony Plain, Alberta in 1894

Johann Schutz Philip Schutz   *   *
Friedrich Schultz
Ludwig Schoepp
Franz Treit   *
Friedrich Ulmer   *
Jacob Ulmer   *
Ludwig Ulmer
Christian Schram
Jacob Schram
Jacob Wendel   *
Heinrich Enders
Ludwig Armbruster
Jacob Mayer
Jacob Mohr
Valentine Mohr
Gottlieb Ducholke   *   *
Martin Ulmer
Ludwig Enders

Lived to celebrate 25th A Anniversary   *

Lived to celebrate 50th Anniversary   * *

Rev. Emil E. Eberhardt D.D. Founding Pastor
Bom - April 20,1870 Died - March 28,1957

St. Matthew Lutheran Church, Stony Plain, Alberta
Pictured above is the 1894 first church and parsonage which was built in 1894. The Pastor and surviving founding members are seen standing here on the occasion of the congregation's 25th Anniversary in 1919 in front of the first church and parsonage.

Early History of St. Matthew

In the late 1800's, a migration of European peoples started with the influx of some German-Austrians into what is now western Canada. For the most part, these new settlers were all farm oriented. Their distribution point was Winnipeg, Manitoba. Among these were some families that settled at Dunmore, a place near Medicine Hat, Alberta. They soon found their new home was located in a semi-arid location. Looking northward, they made their way to Fort Edmonton and then west to Hoffnungsau, later known as Stony Plain, Alberta. There were rumours of lush meadows and plenteous rainfall in that area.

About twenty families found themselves at this new location without a Lutheran pastor. The Rev. F. H. Eggers, a missionary at Great Falls, Montana, found out about their plight. His getting in touch with the Mission Board of the Minnesota District of Synod made it possible to supply these people with a shepherd, in the person of candidate Emil E. Eberhardt. He arrived in Edmonton on Monday, July 29, 1895. He served as pastor at St. Matthew, Stony Plain for over four decades, with the exception of the years 1905-1909.

St. Matthew was considered the "Mother Church of the Great Northwest", as Pastor Eberhardt's Call read, "West of Winnipeg." He was a true missionary. His first obligation was to his congregation, but his travels on his mission duty took him as far as Vancouver on the west coast.

In 1905, Pastor Eberhardt was called to Snohomish, in the State of Washington.

Upon his departure. Pastor H. Reinitz was called by St. Matthew Lutheran Church. After entering the ministry in 1903, Pastor Reinitz served three or four parishes in Manitoba before coming to Stony Plain to start his pastoral duties on June 25, 1905. He was also instrumental in starting a Christian day school at St. Matthew, where he taught five days a week. The school's enrolment soon increased to sixty pupils, with classes being held in the original school- parsonage.

In order to take the heavy load of work off the shoulders of the pastor, the congregation decided to call a teacher. The first teacher called to St. Matthew Lutheran School was A.C. Krieg. He started teaching at Stony Plain in late 1909.

At a meeting on July 25, 1909, Rev. Hermann Reinitz tendered his resignation which was accepted by the congregation.

Members of St. Matthew Lutheran Church, finding themselves without a pastor, turned their attention to Zion Lutheran Church of Snohomish, Washington, U.S.A. Their previous pastor, Emil Eberhardt, declined the first Call extended by the congregation. Upon receiving the second Call, he accepted on August 22, 1909 and returned to Stony Plain in October of that year.

The second pastor to serve the congregation was Rev. H. Reinitz from 1905-1909 at which time Pastor Eberhardt returned.

History At a Glance ....
Background Information:

1889

<u>Early Spring:</u> Approximately 80 families came from Galicia (the Austro-Hungarian Empire) and arrived in Halifax, Nova Scotia.

<u>Summer:</u> These families settled in Dunmore area near Medicine Hat, Alberta.

1891

<u>May:</u> These immigrants moved due to drought and poor crops. Some moved into Saskatchewan, others went north to Edmonton. Here some of the families parted ways. Some went east of Edmonton to Fort Saskatchewan and our forefathers of St. Matthew Lutheran Church settled west of Edmonton in the Stony Plain area.

Pastor F. Pempeit organized St. Matthew's Lutheran Church (Canada Synod of the General Council) at Spruce Grove.

1893

<u>Early Summer:</u> Strife arose in congregation over land dispute. June 8: Twenty families were excommunicated from St. Matthew's Lutheran Church-Canada Synod, Spruce Grove.

100 Years of Blessings

1894

Canada Synod contacted by excommunicated families for visitation. Canada Synod sides with Rev. Pempeit; Missouri Synod contacted for help; Rev. F.H. Eggers, Great Falls, Montana, sent to investigate situation.

<u>May 18:</u> Rev. F. H. Eggers met with group. Decision made to join Missouri Synod. First church service held with Holy Communion. New cemetery dedicated.

<u>May 24:</u> Board of Assignment, Missouri Synod assigned Candidate Emil Eberhardt to Manitoba, Assiniboia (Sask.) and Alberta Territory.

<u>June 27-July 3:</u> At the Minnesota District Convention, Candidate Eberhardt accepts call as Travelling Missionary to Alberta. Commissioned as Travelling Missionary at Bethlehem Lutheran Church, St. Paul, MN.

<u>Early September</u> Rev. Eberhardt arrives in Stony Plain.

<u>October 28:</u> Congregation bought farm from Martin Ulmer.

<u>November 5:</u> St. Matthew Lutheran Church-Missouri Synod, accepted and signed constitution. (20 families, 112 souls). Same meeting, plans were made to build combination church and parsonage.

<u>November 12:</u> Pastor Eberhardt starts confirmation class and also school, (there was no public school)

1895

First recorded burial in cemetery — Daniel Gitzel. (child)

<u>June 10:</u> Pastor Eberhardt and Miss Mary Beiderwieden married in St. Louis. (This marriage was blessed

with 7 children: Emil, Carl, Mary, John, Anne, Lydia and George.)

<u>July 30:</u> Pastor and Mrs. Eberhardt arrived at Stony Plain and moved into combination church and parsonage.

1898
<u>March 19:</u> Special meeting called. Resolution to build a new church. Passed.

1899
<u>May 21:</u> New church was dedicated. Cash outlay — $2800.00

1900
<u>February 18:</u> St. Matthew became self supporting. Had previously been subsidized by Minnesota-Dakota-Montanna District.

1904
Second parsonage built.

1905
<u>March 9:</u> Pastor Eberhardt accepts call to Zion Lutheran Church, Snohomish, Washington, USA.

<u>June 25:</u> Rev. Hermann Reinitz assumes duties as second pastor of St. Matthew.

1909
Teacher A.C. Krieg accepts call as 1st teacher. Starts teaching in fall.

<u>July 25:</u> Pastor Reinitz resigns as pastor.

<u>August 22:</u> Pastor Eberhardt accepted the second call sent to be the pastor at St. Matthew.

<u>October 3:</u> Pastor Eberhardt installed.

St. Matthew instrumental in establishing daughter congregations in the area.

1913
St. Matthew built School #1 on northwest corner of the church property. Cost $1400.00

Teacher A.C. Krieg accepts call to Winnipeg.

<u>July 7:</u> Teacher J. Dobring accepts call and is installed.

1915
Teacher Dobring granted leave of absence due to ill health. (No record that he returned). Student Hildebrandt filled vacancy until school closed.

<u>Fall:</u> The Alberta Department of Education ordered St. Matthew School closed due to intense government feelings.

1921
St. Matthew School #1 re-opened.

<u>August 28:</u> Rev. H.J. Boettcher installed as teacher of St. Matthew School #1.

1922
<u>December 18:</u> St. Matthew School again closed. Was inspected by Alberta Department of Education and declared inefficient but no suggestions were made for improvements.

1923

January 21: Ladies Aid organized.

February 15: Special meeting called because of school closure. Possible emigration from Canada to Mexico.

February 26: Pastor Eberhardt, Henry Goertz and Jacob Miller leave for Mexico to investigate possibility of resettling.

April 10: St. Matthew School reopened.

August 1: Walther League organized.

1924

May 28: Mrs. Mary Eberhardt went to be with her Lord. Bom Aug. 6, 1870 — Died May 28, 1924.

St. Matthew School #2 was built in town of Stony Plain.

Candidate A.H. Golz was called to serve in School #2 along with Rev. Boettcher in School #1.

1927

Teacher Golz resigned before end of school term.

April 25: Candidate Walter Rosnau called and began his teaching duties.

June 27: Pastor Eberhardt married Mrs. Minnie Beiderwieden (nee Spiegelberg). They had one child, Ruth (Hay). John and Carl Beiderwieden are sons of Mrs. Minnie Beiderwieden from her first marriage.

November 13: Rev. H.J. Boettcher accepted call to Grace Lutheran Mission in Edmonton.

Late Fall: Teacher Candidate Philip J. Enders called as teacher of St. Matthew School #2. (Candidate Walter Rosnau at School #1.)

1929

January 16: Resolution passed to hold English service once a month. Rev. V. Ostermann, pastor of Blueberry congregation asked to assist in this area.

February 17: First English service conducted in school #2 in Stony Plain.

1930

Fall: Rev. H. Kuring, new pastor of St. John's Congregation, Blueberry was asked to assist with English service which he did for 12 years. First once a month, then twice a month.

1939

Cairn erected on the site of first church and parsonage.

1942

April 19: Rev. E. Eberhardt tendered his resignation which became effective end of June.

June: Concordia Seminary of St. Louis, Missouri bestowed the Honorary Degree of Doctor of Divinity upon Dr. E. Eberhardt for outstanding work in the Alberta-British Columbia District.

November 1: Rev. G. H. Raedeke installed as pastor of St. Matthew.

Sunday School classes revived by Pastor Raedeke. (First attempted in 1922-1923).

1943

March 19: Sgt. Walter Foerster, member of St. Matthew congregation died for his country in World War II. (45 members of St. Matthew congregation were in active duty during World War II).

1944

January: St Matthew congregation resolved to start a church building fund.

1946

June 30: Teacher Walter Rosnau leaves teaching profession.

Miss Margaret Armbruster (Shwed) was engaged as teacher of St. Matthew School #1 (country).

October: Rev. G.H. Raedeke accepts a call to Ottawa, Ontario. Teacher Philip J. Enders accepts call to Ottawa, Ontario.

Miss Anne K. Miller was engaged as teacher of St. Matthew School # 2 (town)

December 15: Rev. Philip J. Janz was installed as pastor of St. Matthew Lutheran Church.

1947

New parsonage built in town of Stony Plain.

Congregation farm sold to Otto C. Hennig.

May 11: Final plans for a new church to be built in the Town of Stony Plain were submitted to the congregation.

May 27: St. Matthew Altar Guild was organized.

1949

October 30: New church building dedicated.

1954

January: Lutheran Women's Missionary League (LWML) was organized.

Fall: Rev. Philip Janz accepts call to Plainview, Nebraska.

November 14: New school (present building) dedicated. Dr. H.J. Boettcher, Chicago, guest speaker.

Mrs. Elizabeth Komberger engaged as 3rd teacher.

Miss Anne Miller accepted the position of principal (1954-1958).

1955

April: St. Matthew School #1 sold.

July 24: Rev. Arthur Gehring installed as pastor of St. Matthew Lutheran Church.

Zion Lutheran Church, Inga congregation, received into membership of St. Matthew.

November 17: Lutheran Laymen's League organized.

1956

Evangelism Committee organized.

1957

March 28: Dr. Emil Eberhardt went to be with his Lord.

1958
St. Matthew School #2 sold.

July: Walter Kupsch was called as principal (1958-1974).

1959
September 4: 4th classroom at school opened; (for list of teachers see 90th History Book.)

Bible Class program implemented.

1960
January 13: Mrs. Minnie Eberhardt departed this life. (Dr Emil Eberhardt's 2nd wife).

1961
February 9: Parent Teacher-League organized.

Two more classrooms added to school.

50th Anniversary of St. Matthew Lutheran School. (50 full years of operation).

1965
Vacation Bible School organized.

1967
July 23: Miniature church at cemetery dedicated.

December First grant received for school.

1969
Kindergarten classes started at school.

1972
(1972-1973) Paul Langohr served as Vicar.

November 26: Rev. Arthur Gehring was called to be with his Lord.

Rev. Walter Koehler served as Vacancy Pastor.

Rev. Carl Baron helped with St. Matthew German services, as needed, for many years.

1973
July 22: Rev. William Ney was installed as pastor.

1974
January: Rev. Walter Schoepp was installed as associate pastor.

July: Rev. William Ney accepted Call to Concordia College at Ann Arbor, Michigan.

Walter Kupsch resigned his position as teacher and principal from St. Matthew School.

William Sandau became principal of our school. (1974-1983)

100% funding through grants was received by our school for Kindergarten.

August: Building program of gym, classroom, offices and foyer was begun at school.

1975

June 1: Liz Graul became full time parish worker. (1975-1977)

1976
May 2: The gym and new addition to school were dedicated.

1977
January 30: Liz Graul leaves St. Matthew.

Ron Wesley served as Vicar. (1977-1978)

1978
Mike Colbeck served as Vicar. (1978-1979)

Ken Olson, Director of Christian Education, was installed.

1979
Terry Richardson served as Vicar. (1979-1980)

1980
Dan Hansard served as Vicar. (1980-1981)

1981
May: Rev. Walter Schoepp accepted a call to Riverbend, Edmonton.

Jim Schnarr served as Vicar. (1981-1982)

Ken Olson left our congregation.

November 8: Rev. Murvyn Kentel was installed as pastor.

1982
October3: Rev. Jim Schnarr was installed as associate pastor.

1983
William Sandau accepted a call to Hayward, California.

500th Anniversary of Martin Luther's Birthday celebrated.
Town of Stony Plain celebrated 75th Anniversary.

New church sign installed.

Daryl Becker accepted position of principal at school. (1983-1987)

1984
April: Rev. Jim Schnarr accepted call to Pickering, Ontario.

September: Rev. Harold Witte was installed as associate pastor.

St. Matthew Lutheran Church celebrated 90th Anniversary.

Young Mom's was organized.

1985
January 27:
The congregation resolved to add grade 9 to the school's junior high department in the 1985-1986 school year.

Bob Enders and Ivan Boles were selected to serve as delegate and alternate to the Albert-British Columbia District Convention.

April 27:
The congregation approved the organization of a building fund, building committee and building finance committee.

June 9:
The recommendation to open a playschool in September of 1985 was approved.

November 5:
The congregation passed a resolution to plan and construct an addition to the existing church building.

1986
January 7:
Daryl Becker submitted his resignation as principal, desiring to return to teaching full time.

January 26:
St. Matthew Evangelical Lutheran Church expressed its intent to seek membership in Lutheran Church-Canada at its founding convention.

April 6:
Architect Norbert Lemermeyer was instructed by the congregation to proceed with the design development stage of building, upon acceptance of the schematics presented at this meeting.

April 29:
J. Schuknecht was called to teach - declined.

June 1:
Wendy Fraser was called to teach - accepted. •

William Quast was offered the position of teacher/principal - declined.

July 6:
Gerald Nast was called as teacher/principal - declined.

August 27:
Alvin Clark was contracted to serve as teacher/principal for the 1986-1987 school term.

Debra Stresman was contracted to serve as playschool coordinator/teacher.

September 27:
Teacher Sue Yelden was granted a 6-month sabbatical leave, January to June, 1987.

School celebrated 75th Anniversary.

Stephen Ministry program initiated by Bob Enders.

Building Committee formed for addition to church.

1987
January 25:
A report was received from the building committee formed for the completion of the building project. Members of this committee were John Adam, John Armbruster, Ivan Boles, Murray Framingham, Roland Hennig, Richard Mohr, William Quast, Stan Shwed, Glenn Stresman and pastors as ex-officio.

German services were changed to only 2 Sundays per month.

March 8:
The congregation decided to become its own general contractor and hire a project manager to oversee the construction, and that construction could begin when the congregation holds $500,000.00 in the bank. Authority was granted for the building committee to form a limited company/building society for the purpose of the construction project.

May 3:
The Constitution Review Committee submitted their report.

May 31:
Teaching contracts were renewed for Alvin Clark, Brenda Rockney and Rosalyn Rosher.

July 26:
Daryl Becker submitted his resignation after accepting a call to Zion Lutheran School, Cloverdale, B.C.

Teaching contracts were offered to Bev Rosnau, Todd Wandio and Ed Schnellert.

September 13:
Pastor Kentel accepted a call from the Alberta-British Columbia District to establish a mission in Calgary. The congregation extended a call to Rev. Donald Koch as associate pastor - declined.

September 20:
Discussions on the review of the constitution continued.

November 22:
Teaching calls were extended to Elly van den Brande and Marilyn Quast - accepted.

December 9:
A vote to apply for membership in Lutheran Church-Canada was carried unanimously. John Armbruster and Don Whitlock were selected delegate and alternate.

A pastoral call was extended to Rev. James Schuelke - declined.

Alvin Clark accepts position as principal. (1987-1988)

Bryan Rosnau serves us as seminarian.

Rev. Lester Gierach helps us with our German services.

1988
January 17:
The revised constitution was accepted, with the congregational by-laws still under discussion.

February 28:
A pastoral call was extended to Rev. Robert Krestick - declined.

March 20:
The revised constitution and by-laws were forwarded to Alberta-British Columbia District and to the government of Alberta, under the Societies Act

June 12:
A pastoral call to Rev. Donald Schiemann to serve as associate pastor was extended - accepted.

Teacher Marilyn Quast submitted her resignation. A call to Eldon Nast to serve as teacher/principal was declined. Alvin Clark resigns as principal.

July 31:
A call was extended to Glen Zorn to serve as teacher/principal - declined.

A teaching contract to serve as half-time kindergarten teacher was offered to Carolynne Herfindahl.

October 16:
Rev. Don Schiemann was installed as associate pastor.

December 4:
April 2, 1989 was set for the official ground-breaking service for the addition to the church with actual construction to commence on April 3,1989.

Gordon Heselton serves as seminarian.

Lutheran Church-Canada becomes a reality.

1989
January 29:
A call to teach, including an appointment to serve as principal, was extended to Wendy Fraser - accepted.

The revised constitution of St. Matthew Evangelical Lutheran Church, as accepted and ratified by the constitution committee and board of directors of Alberta-British Columbia District, was adopted by the congregation. The newly adopted constitution took effect immediately, and the members present at this meeting were given the opportunity to sign the constitution. The Constitution

Review Committee was dismissed with thanks for their diligence.

April 2:
Ground breaking for church addition.

July 30:
The teaching contract signed by Eric Ladoski was ratified.

A teaching call was extended to Jonathan Stanfel - accepted.

September 24:
The congregation announced its commitment to the organization of a "Lutheran Open House Mission", to be held in September of 1990.

October 17:
A 100th Anniversary Committee was established.

Project Manager is hired for church building project.

Parsonage dismantled.

1990
June 17:
A joyful service of dedication of the addition to the church facility was held.

August 19:
A teaching contract was offered to Mrs. Arlyn Belden.

September 30:
A teaching call to Rosalyn Rosher, who had recently completed the colloquy program, was extended - accepted.

A four-day Lutheran Open House was hosted, wrapping up months of preparation, including a rally, surveys, visits and publicity. Rev. Wallace Schulz, speaker for the Lutheran Hour, served as guest speaker.

December
Pastor Witte received and accepted a call to All Saints Lutheran Church in Edmonton. His last Sunday in St. Matthew's service was January 27,1991.

Bruce Corson serves as seminarian. (1990-1991).

1991
March 10:
A pastoral call extended to Rev. Mark Ruf was declined.

May-August:
Concordia Lutheran Seminary student Jack Stoop served as summer vicar.

May 29:
A pastoral call extended to Rev. Robert Schulze was declined.

June:
Pastor Schiemann and Rev. Bill Ney travelled to the USSR as part of a group conducting mission work.

July 14:
Contracts were offered to new teachers Bev Adam, Anika Ladoski and Corinne Nowoczin.

August 25:
A pastoral call to Rev. James Scholz was declined.

October 20:
A pastoral call to Rev. Roger Sedlmayr, as associate pastor, was accepted.

November 26:
Teaching calls were extended to Arlyn Belden and Corinne Nowoczin - accepted.

Benno Dreger serves us as Seminarian. (1991-1992).

1992
February 2:
Rev. Roger Sedlmayr is installed as associate pastor.

April 5:
CBC's "Meeting Place" recorded a Palm Sunday service that was aired the next week.

September 20:
The congregation adopted the Youth Ukraine Mission as a congregational mission project for 1992-1993.

Finance Management Committee appointed.

1993
January 31:
A decision was made to require payment of school tuition fees by both congregational members as well as

non-members.

February:
German service was discontinued.

March:
Pastor Schiemann, Rev. Bill Ney and a group of young people, many of them from the congregation, travelled to Ukraine on a youth mission.

April 20:
Church council ratified the establishment of the St. Matthew Evangelical Lutheran Church Active Endowment Fund, to be managed by Alberta-British Columbia District.

August 17:
Pastor Don Schiemann was asked to conduct mission work in Cameroon in January of 1994.

December 15:
Pastor Don Schiemann received the call to be Mission Executive of the Alberta-British Columbia District - accepted.

Jonathan Kraemer and Ken Edel served us as our seminarians. (1993-1994)

1994
A Year of Celebrations

January 19:
(Centennial Event) Concordia College Choir

February 6:
(Voters) Pastor Schiemann was granted a peaceful release from his call

February 12:
(Centennial Event) Tea and bake sale

February 15:
(Council) A new computer system, including the program LCIS 2000 (Lutheran Church Information System 2000) will be purchased for keeping congregational records.

March 11:
(Centennial Event) Christian singing group

April 24:
(Voters) Called Pastor Robert Willie as Associate Pastor- declined. Established a Centennial Thank Offering

April 26:
(Centennial Event) Fashion show and ice cream social

April 29:
(Centennial Event) St. Matthew School concert

May 10:
(Centennial Event) St. Matthew School concert

May 29:
(Voters) Established the position of congregational business administrator

June 3-6:
(Centennial Event) Hosted the 43rd District Convention of The Alberta-British Columbia District

June 3:
Opening Service - St. Matthew Lutheran Church

June 4:
Convention Sessions begin

June 5:
Mission Festival

June 26:
(Voters) Called Rev. William Heine as Associate Pastor - accepted

July 8-10:
(Centennial Event) Ball Tournament

August 21:
(Centennial Event) Picnic and fun (cancelled)

September 10:
(Centennial Event) Ethnic supper

September 26:
(Voters) Ratify teaching contracts for 1994-1995 school year
       Bev Adam -1/2 time
       Cliff Opheim - 1/2 time
       Eric Ladoski - full time
       Wendy Robinson - full time

October 10:
(Centennial Event) St. Matthew School concert

November 6:
(Centennial Event) St. Matthew 100th Anniversary Celebration

December 21:
(Centennial Event) Sunday school program

Thank and Praise God for 100 Years of Blessings

"History at A Glance" was compiled by:
-Marvin and Rose Hennig (Covering from 1889 - 1993)
-Carol Birrell (Covering from 1985 - 1994)

Year of Celebrations was compiled by:
-Carol Birrell (including the congregational highlights)
-Roland Hennig (including the events)

Reference Sources Used:
1) Baron, Eric J. (1984). Lutheran, St. Matthew A Ninety Year History, Edmonton: Uvisoco Publishing: Edmonton, Alberta.

2) Raedeke, G. H. (1944). <u>Fiftieth Anniversary of St. Matthew's Evangelical Lutheran Church</u>

3) Schwermann, Albert H. (1962). Vol. XXXIV, No. 4, <u>Concordia Historical Institute Quarterly,</u> "The Life and Times of Emil E. Eberhardt", Edmonton: Concordia College Publishing.

4) Congregational Minutes, St. Matthew Lutheran Church, Stony Plain, AB.

5) Anniversary committee Minutes, St. Matthew Lutheran Church, Stony Plain, AB.

The Editors for the above compilations to <u>History At A Glance</u> were Roland Hennig and Eric Baron.

This Excerpt taken from the Fiftieth Anniversary Book, Zion Evangelical Lutheran Church, Snohomish, Washington, USA 1942.

"For a whole year the congregation was without a regular pastor, during which time Mr. Koshe conducted reading services almost every Sunday, and also made many sick visits. The congregation was obliged to call no less than nine times before it finally received a new shepherd in the person of Pastor E. Eberhardt of St. Matthew, Stony Plain, Alberta, Canada, who arrived in the spring of 1905.

During the pastorate of Rev. Eberhardt, the congregation continued to grow, passing the 400 mark. The school grew correspondingly so that Pastor Eberhardt was obliged to assist for a time. To relieve him of this work, a lady teacher was employed for two years. The congregation then resolved to call a second teacher. Candidate H.B. Mantey, a graduate of our teachers' seminary at Seward, Nebraska, received the call and entered upon his work in the fall of 1909, teaching the four lower grades until 1918, when he accepted a call to Everett.

In September, 1909, Pastor Eberhardt received a call from his former congregation in Stony Plain, Alberta, Canada, which he accepted."

Pictured above is Zion Lutheran Church, Snohomish, Washington, USA where Pastor Eberhardt preached for a period of four years during his absence from Stony Plain.

1

Rev. Henry Mohr

Rev. Henry Mohr, son of Valentine and Philipina Mohr, was bom at Stony Plain, Alberta on September 16, 1892. He received his early training in this greatest of Missouri Lutheran communities in Canada. In the year 1908, he entered our college at St. Paul, Minnesota as one of the first two recruits to the Army of the Lord from Alberta. He completed his preparatory course in the year 1914, and entered the seminary at St. Louis, Missouri in the fall of that same year. After three years of study he received and accepted a Call to Pincher Creek, Alberta.

He faithfully served this and a sister congregation for one and a half years until he was stricken with influenza. He died in the hospital at Pincher Creek, on January 12, 1919. He died cheerfully, confiding in Him whom he had confessed. He was not married. He was predeceased by his parents, and survived by four brothers and three sisters. Funeral services were held at Pincher Creek on January 14, and at Stony Plain on January 17, with Rev. Emil Eberhardt as one of the participants. Rev. Mohr lies buried at St. Matthew Lutheran Cemetery.

Rev. Henry Mohr one of the earliest sons of St. Matthew Congregation who served in southern Alberta until his premature death.

The parents Valentine and Philipina Mohr with Pastor Mohr's brothers Philip and Valentine Jr. and sisters-in-law.

The grandfather and grandmother Mohr to Pastor Mohr. His aunt and father (young boy) are in the back row.

C. F. W. Walther

In August of 1844, C. E W. Walther was pastor of the German Evangelical- Lutheran Congregation of the unaltered Augsburg Confession in St. Louis, Missouri. He made known that he had the wish to publish a church periodical to serve Lutherans in Missouri and Illinois. He presented his plan to the members of his congregation. He also made his wish known to other congregations.

September 7, 1844, the first edition of "Der Lutheraner" appeared. He never expected the result that was achieved. He was officially made editor by the publishers of the Evangelical Lutheran Synod of Missouri, Ohio and other states.

Over twenty years he remained editor of this periodical. Later he became less active in the production of the periodical. In total he worked 42 years

with "Der Lutheraner". C. F. W. Walther went to be with His Lord on May 7, 1887.

This is a translation from the German work found in "Amerikanisher Kalendar fur deutche Lutheraner 1944", p. 22-23.

Dr C.F.W. Walther was the founder of the Walther League in the United States and Canada.

Pastor G. H. Raedeke with members of 1944 Walther League

The History of the International Walther League

The Walther League (youth organization of the former Synodical* Conference, with most societies in LCMS). Organized May 23, 1893, at Trinity Church, Buffalo, N.Y. The name Walther Liga (from C.F. W. Walther*) was adopted 1894. the constitution of the Walther League stated: "The purpose of this association shall be to help young people grow as Christians through WORSHIP - building a stronger faith in the Triune God: EDUCATION - discovering the will of God for their daily life: SERVICE - responding to the needs of all men; RECREATION - keeping the joy of Christ in all activities; FELLOWSHIP - finding the power of belonging to others in Christ."

The League involved youth in worship, leadership training schools, camping, writing and publishing, various training projects of service (welfare), missions, vocational guidance, recruitment for church professions, opportunities for practical experience in roles of leadership, and opportunities for a wider circle of fellowship than the home parish. It had it own headquarters building, paid for by the young people, erected in 1942 in Chicago.

The League also sponsored the Wheat* Ridge Foundation, whose directors were elected annually by the international exhibition building for the Walther League. The supports sanitoria and hospitals in Wheat Ridge (Colorado), Japan, India, Hong Kong, New Guinea, and Nigeria, in addition to regular support of other Lutheran welfare agencies in the United States and Canada. It also contributes to the support of religious, education and scientific projects. Financial support is given through an annual Wheat Ridge seals campaign at Christmas.

Walther League publications included the *Walther League Messenger* (Walter A. Maier*, editor); the *Workers Quarterly* (Alfred P. Klausler, editor), a quarterly topic discussion and program guide for societies; *Arena* (Alfred P. Klausler, editor), a monthly magazine for young adults; and *Spirit* (Walter Riess, editor), a monthly magazine for teenagers.

Taken from: Lutheran Cyclopedia, Erwin L Lueker, Editor, Concordia Publishing House, St. Louis, MO, 1954, p. 836

The History of the Stony Plain Walther League

by Walter Rosnau

The Walther League was the youth organization of the Lutheran Church- Missouri Synod, organized on May 23, 1893 and named after Dr. C.F.W. Walther, the first president of the Lutheran Church.

The purpose of the organization was to help the young people grow in Christ through worship - building a strong faith; education - discovering the will of God for their daily living; service - responding to the needs of all men; recreation - keeping the joy of Christ in all activities; and fellowship - finding the power of belonging to others in Christ.

The league involved youth in worship, leadership training schools, camping, writing, publishing, various training projects of service, welfare, missions, occasional guidance and recruitment in roles of leadership. It also provided a wider circle of fellowship than the home parish.

It's headquarters were in Chicago in a building owned and paid for by the membership. The Walther League Messenger and the Worker's Quarterly were published by the League to assist the local societies. In 1969, Synod appointed a Board for Youth Ministry which took over the work of the League.

During the years of its existence, it flourished and spread throughout United States and also into Canada. At the convention of the Alberta - British Columbia District of the Lutheran Church at Bruderheim in 1924, the District Walther League was organized. The district was divided into zones. These zones met for spring and fall rallies. The entire district met for a winter conference and a district convention in summer. The members from the League at St. Matthew, Stony Plain took a very active part in the local society and also at the district level. Numerous district offices were held by members from St. Matthew. The first district president was Miss Emelia Miller from Stony Plain (later the wife of Rev. B.E. Behrends).

The district sponsored many Summer Camps at different locations in the Alberta - British Columbia District Talent quests were conducted in connection with the Winter Conference. They included art, handicraft, writing, oratoiy, music, singing, etc.

The local Walther League was active in many phases of the congregation, especially among the youth. Meetings were held twice a month. Bible study and a topic discussion were a must at every meeting. Then followed an evening of games, entertainment, fellowship and a lunch. Numerous hikes, outings, sleigh rides, skating parties on a lake by a large bonfire, camping and ice fishing (for the hardy type) were events that were well attended and enjoyed. There was strong emphasis on recreation. The League encouraged tennis. Two tennis courts were available; one on the school grounds at St. Matthew #1 School and the private court belonging to George Oppertshauser. A men's and a ladies' basketball team also played in the district league during the years of its existence. For years the Walther League baseball team had an enviable record against the teams from the surrounding communities and districts.

During the 30's and 40's the annual 3-act plays produced by the **21**

Walther Leaguers were an event to which the community looked forward. Some of them were presented in other towns and at Concordia College, Edmonton.

Other major undertakings were: window displays, Christmas manger scene, distribution of tracts, supporting the Lutheran Hour over radio, the annual reunion for the newly confirmed, and Christmas and Hallowe'en parties.

Many a youth was kept from being lost to the church by his contact with, and the support of, the members of the League. During World War II, many of the Leaguers joined the armed forces. The Leaguers remaining at home kept in touch with them through letters, news bulletins, parcels of "goodies" and clothing.

One of the members, Sgt. Walter Foerster, paid the supreme sacrifice on March 19, 1943. The St. Matthew Leaguers dedicated a stained glass window in his memory. It is the window in the north wall of the stone church. They also erected a stone cairn marking the location of the first house of worship of St. Matthew congregation dedicated July, 1895. This cairn is in the south end of the cemetery.

Over the years, the Walther League has been a blessing to the church. Many a romance had its beginning at a summer camp, winter conference, summer convention, fall or spring rally, reunion or other fellowship events. Where this culminated in a marriage of two Christian young people, it was a blessing to the family, the church and society.

The founding of the Walther League held at Bruderheim, Alberta in 1924.

St. Matthew Young People's group at the convention of the Walther League held at Edmonds Beach, 1929.

Organized May. 23. 1893.

WALTHER LEAGUE

OF THE

EVANGELICAL LUTHERAN SYNODICAL CONFERENCE

PRO ARIS ET FOGIS

Certificate No. 1312

St. Matthew Walther League

Stony Plain, Alberta, Canada was accepted

February 6th 1924 as a member of the

Walther League, in accordance with the constitution.

The Executive Board.

E. W. Klein

Secretary

WALTHER LEAGUE

LEAGUE

ORGANIZED MAY 23, 1893

CHARTER NO. 1464

OF THE

Evangelical Lutheran Synodical Conference

PRO ARIS ET FOCIS

St. Matthew Jr. W. L.

Stony Plain, Alberta was accepted

as a member of the Walther League

in accordance with the Constitution

June 5 19 44   THE INTERNATIONAL WALTHER LEAGUE

Secretary of the Executive Board

The Hundredth Anniversary Committee

In Recognition of the Above:
(Front Row L-R) Rev. Don Schiemann, Eric Baron, Rose Hennig, Roland Hennig
(Second Row L-R) Walter Doern, Pastor Roger Sedlmayr, Walter Kupsch, Dean Litzenberger. Absent from our photo was Pastor William Heine, Joan Denninger, Gail Howelett, and Anika Ladoski.

The Chairman's Summary For The Anniversary Year

By Roland Hennig

In these words I will now summarize my perspective of our 100th anniversary.

We began the year 1994 with a great deal of anxiety and expectation. Were we ready to carry out the plans which were made over the past few years to celebrate our 100th anniversary? Our monthly events started in January with Concordia College Choir and were carried on during the course of the year. Our last event was held in December, a few days prior to Christmas, and put on by the children of our Sunday School. (A complete list of monthly events is printed elsewhere in this book under History at a Glance.)

As these functions were carried out, the time came when we were to reach our goal which was set in February of 1990 - to celebrate the 100th anniversary of St. Matthew Lutheran Church.

November 6, 1994 the anniversary day had now come. As we humbly came before our Heavenly Father to rejoice, give thanks and sing praises to Him, and Him alone, who has made this day possible. To Him be all honor and glory. Yes, 100 years! By the Grace of God we reached this blessed and wonderful milestone on November 6th. What a privilege and honor to be a part of it! None of us will ever again witness another event like the 100th anniversary here at St. Matthew.

We are here only by the Grace of God, not of our own merit or worthiness. Not because of what we have done, but what He has done for us!

The climax to this great celebration began with the Divine Service of worship which began at 10:00 A.M. It included the celebration of Holy Communion presided over by Pastor Roger Sedlmayr and assisted by Pastor William Heine.

The day continued with the Service of Praise and Thanksgiving which began at 3:30 P.M. Pastor Heine presiding and assisting was Pastor Sedlmayr.

Our guest speaker, Rev. Carl Beiderwieden, step-son of our founding pastor Rev. Dr. Emil Eberhardt, brought us a challenging sermon. Our former pastor, Rev. Murvyn Kentel delivered a short German message.

After the service, special greetings were brought to us from pastors of sister congregations, dignitaries and friends.

Following the afternoon service of thanksgiving, a dinner was held at St. © ©' Matthew Lutheran School for all our church members, guests and friends who were present. A wonderful time of praise and fellowship was shared and experienced by everyone present.

Finally, the past is history and we shall reflect upon this for lessons to learn from. We shall not forget the great © © challenges, hardships, moments of glory and victories that were once experienced by our forefathers and relived in our hearts and minds this day as a memorial to their faithfulness to God our Creator.

Although many uncertainties lie before us, we will face our challenges and obstacles with the same courage and faith that our forefathers had. The lessons they taught us, by their Christian example during these preceding one hundred years, can only be measured by the strength of our faith in and loyalty to Christ our Saviour and risen Lord.

Just as God was their refuge and sure defence, he will no less be ours today by renewing our commitment to Him. He will never leave us nor forsake us. This is His promise to all His believing people to the end of time. This is our confession. This we believe. Thanks be to God!

A Message from the Anniversary Committee

by Roland Hennig

As 1993 draws to a close, we look forward to celebrating the birth of our risen Saviour, which took place almost 2,000 years ago. Also at this time, we are looking forward to another celebration, the 100th anniversary of St Matthew congregation. What a blessing and privilege for those of us who are here today and will be in a year from now. At that time, God willing, we will gather as a large family of believers in Chnst, to give praise and thanksgiving to our Heavenly Father for His innumerable blessings bestowed upon us over a century.

At the Alberta-British Columbia District Convention in May of 1988, it was resolved to hold a "Season of Jubilee" from 1994-1996 during which time the following anniversaries will be observed:

1994

-The 100th Anniversary of the arrival of the first Lutheran Church-Missouri Synod missionary in our district (Rev. Emil Eberhardt);
-The establishment of the first congregation - St. Matthew, Stony Plain, Alberta;
-The 100th Anniversary of the establishment of Concordia Lutheran Seminary.

1995

-The 100th Anniversary of the construction of the first church building in our district (St. Matthew, Stony Plain, Alberta).

1996

-The 75th Anniversary of the formation of the Alberta-British Columbia District;
-The 75th Anniversary of the establishment of Concordia College, Edmonton, Alberta.

Our committee was formed in February of 1990, and since then has been working and planning activities starting in January of 1994. An event will be offered each month throughout the year by organizations, groups, boards and committees, etc. A complete list of activities will be posted for all to see, and each event will be advertised a month ahead of time.

Two functions of special interest to our people, besides our special anniversary service in November, are the hosting of both the Placement Service of Concordia Lutheran Seminary in April and the Opening Service of the Alberta-British Columbia District Convention in June.

The sale of commemorative items is well under way. There are available bone china plates, T-shirts, mugs, and recently added, lapel pins. We encourage our members to pick up some of these souvenir items. If we run out, some can be re-ordered. A limited supply of plates is available, and we encourage you to get yours soon. We will not be placing another order for plates.

Dear members of St. Matthew, we should consider it an honour and a privilege to be a part of the celebrations of the "Season of Jubilee". We hope and pray that all of our members will take this time of celebration to heart and participate in as many functions as possible.

As was mentioned some time ago, we are looking for pictures, write-ups, annual reports, and a history of our congregation. If anyone has any of these and would like to donate or loan them to be put on display, we would greatly appreciate it. Our first display will be shown in January and will pertain to the first ten-year history of 1894 to 1904.

As we go forward into our year of celebration, may God be with us to watch over us, to guide and protect us as He did our forefathers over the past century.

As this report was given at the close of 1993, on the threshold of a new year which would see the beginning and the end of an historic celebration to our 100th anniversary, the chairman made the above report.

Centennial Monthly Events:

January 19 - Concordia College Choir
February 12 - Tea and Bake Sale
March 11 - Christian singing group
April 26 - Fashion show and ice cream social
April 29 - Placement service - Concordia Seminary graduates
May 10 - St. Matthew School concert
June 3 - A-BC District Convention Opening Service
June 5 - Mission Festival
July 8-10 - Ball tournament
August 21 - Picnic and fun (cancelled)
September 10 - Ethnic supper
September 11 - 100th Anniversary congregation picture taken
October 10 - St. Matthew School concert
November 5, 100th ANNIVERSARY CELEBRATION!
    10:00 am Communion Service
    3:00 pm Festive Service of Thanksgiving and Praise followed by dinner and fellowship
December 21 - Sunday School Christmas Program

Several other projects were undertaken by our committee with the help of the sub-committees. They included:

1. A pastor picture display, depicting all the pastors and their years of service to our congregation, placed on permanent display in the narthex of our church.

2. A pictorial book of our membership - a 3rd in a series.

3. Our last event which took place after the anniversary was held a few days prior to Christmas. This program was put on by the children of our Sunday School.

4. Very early in the year our committee felt it would be fitting to initiate a Centennial Thankoffering in connection with our anniversary celebration. This was to give our membership the opportunity to give praise and thanks to our Heavenly Father for His endless blessings showered upon our congregation for over a century. This offering was to be over and above our regular giving patterns. A committee was formed and a program was set forth to lead our people in this direction.

Hundredth Anniversary
Sub Committee
A Sequel to "Lutheran, St. Matthew, Stony Plain, Alberta"

We Held our preliminary meeting on the evening of Wednesday, February 24, 1993. Our committee was formed to gather the historical data and events of the past decade and produce a publication for this time period, since there had been a book published covering the previous ninety years. The current committee consisted of Roland C. Hennig and Eric J. Baron. They met no less than eighteen times with the publisher Reuben Bauer, who showed great proficiency in this occupation. We thank him for his help.

At times we met at members residences, and at times at a restaurant. There we usually had a coffee while we discussed our next move. On one occasion one of the members spilled a cup of coffee, which caused quite a stir, as valuable papers could have been ruined. Not all was lost and our meeting continued.

We would like to thank the proof readers for their diligent work in correcting spelling errors, punctuation, etc. Recognition should be given to many more contributors in work and time, in order to bring this book into fruition.

The pastors were also helpful when asked questions about the book project and they gave us spiritual profiles with their entries. Their input will be much appreciated and will add greatly to the interest in this book.

"Pictures speak louder than words". This saying has been in existence for centuries. The ancient Egyptians had murals in their pyramids which were painted or drawn in honor of their departed rulers. St. Matthew Lutheran Church thousands of years later, published a book and requested for pictures of the last hundred years. We received virtually hundreds of pictures. There are edited according to the story in the write-up. To all who provided pictures a big "thank you".

Wishing St. Matthew God's Blessings and many more centuries.

Contributed by: Eric J. Baron

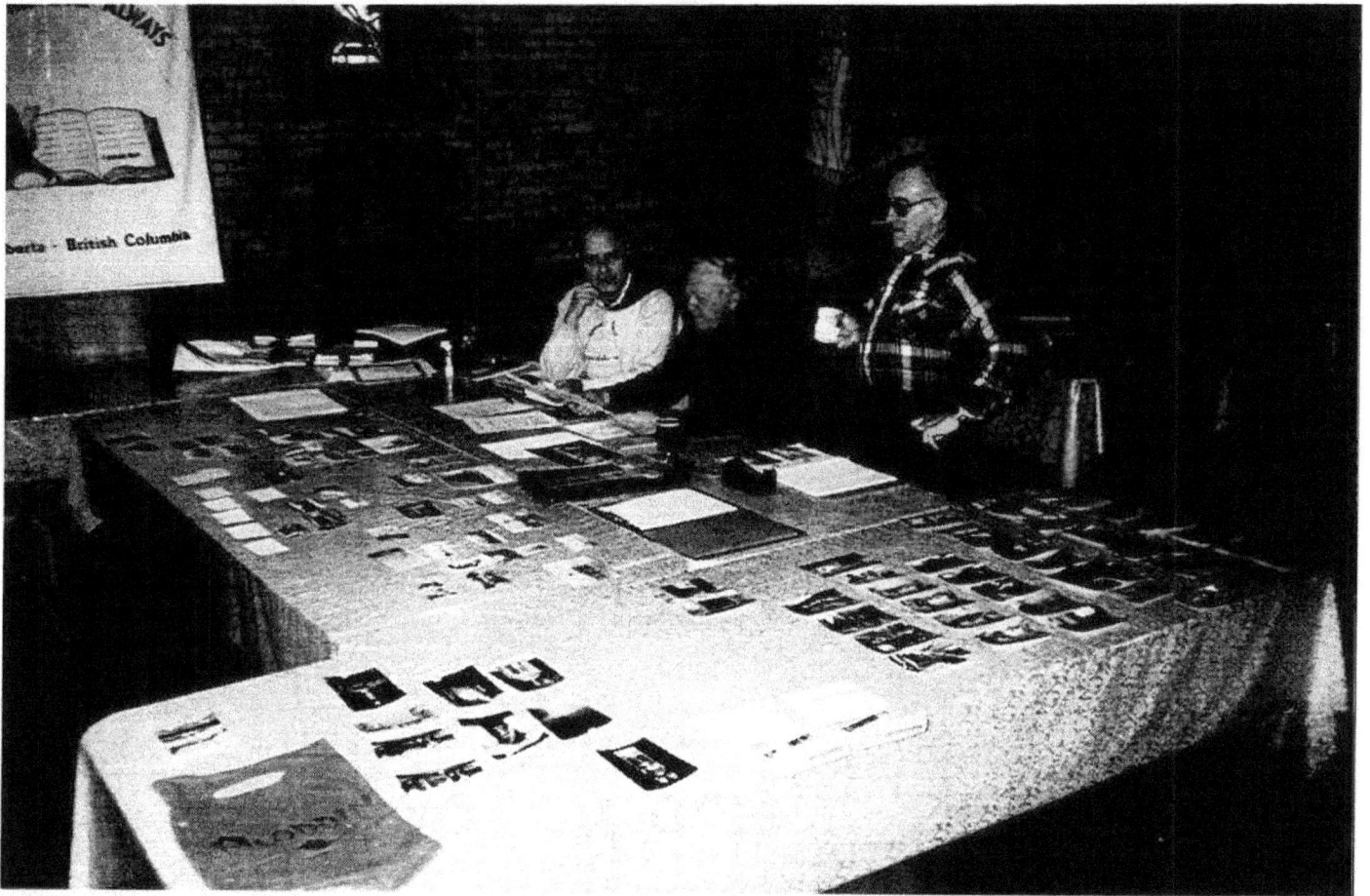

Book Sub-Committee At Work This one hundredth anniversary was culminated in the collection of stories and pictures. This collection is gathered up in the pages of this book which is produced by the sub-committee consisting of Roland Hennig (Chairman of the 100th Anniversary Committee) and Eric Baron (author of the previous 90th Anniversary history publication. St. Matthew Lutheran Church commissioned Reuben Bauer (printer and publisher of these histories) to consult for one of the most valuable published histories of the Lutheran Church Canada. Left to right in the above photo are Reuben Bauer, Roland Hennig and Eric Baron.

The Setting For the One Hundredth Anniversary Day Service

The Altar in the new sanctuary of St. Matthew Lutheran Church.
The hundredth anniversary of St. Matthew took place in this beautiful new house of praise and worship on Sunday, November 6, 1994. The occasion marked a major event in the life of the church's history, the founding of St. Matthew Lutheran Church in Stony Plain, Alberta one hundred years previous.

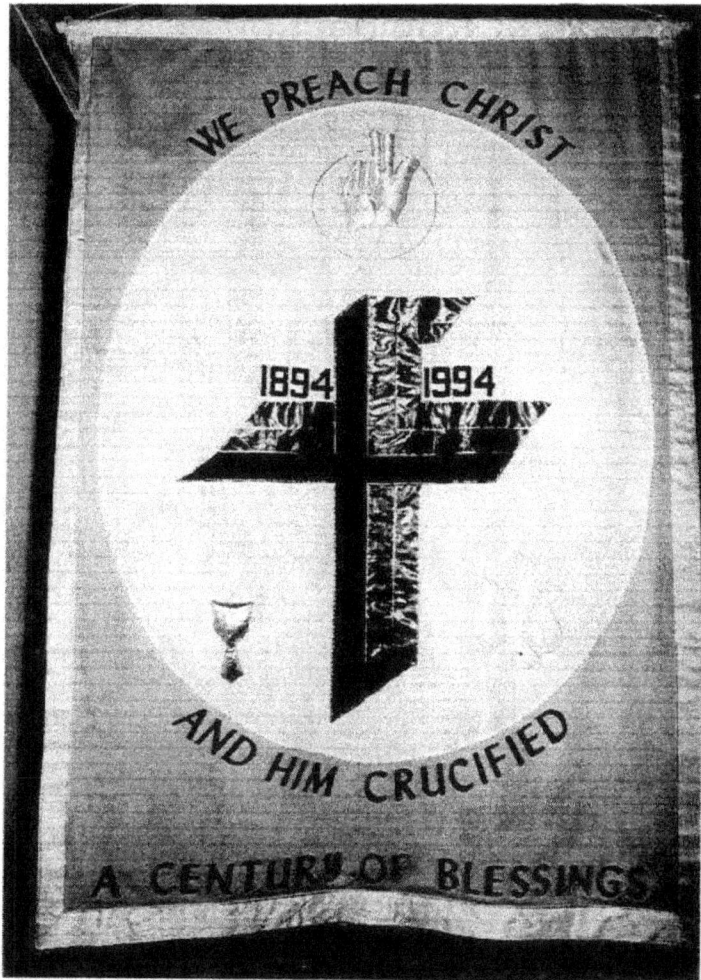

These two banners were the winning entries selected from a competition which saw numerous other very beautiful hand-made submissions.

Additional Banners Submitted for Competition

Matthew-28:19-20

WE PREACH CHRIST
AND HIM CRUCIFIED

1884 ~ 1994

The Day of Celebration, November 6, 1994

The flag bearer leads the procession at the opening day of celebration with the Christian Flag.

The second flag bearer is seen here carrying the Flag of Canada followed by the Christian in banners designed for this historic occasion and used the procession.

Closing the procession as they entered the sanctuary were the four presiding pastors during this special service.

The presiding pastors with the guest speakers. (L-R) Rev. M. Kentel (German Message), Rev. R. Sedlmayr (Senior Pastor at St. Matthew), Rev. William Heine (Associate Pastor at St. Matthew) and Rev. C. Beiderwieden (step-son of the founding pastor Dr. E. Eberhardt) who delivered the English message.

One Hundredth Anniversary
St. Matthew Evangelical Lutheran Church
November 06, 1994

Presentations and Greetings

10:00 a.m. Divine Service

Rev. Walt and Em Schoepp will present a hand crafted model of the 1899 church to the members of St. Matthew. This model was made by Mrs. Elsie Ulmer of Salmon Arm, British Columbia. There are two music boxes mounted in the church model. They play "How Great Thou Art" and "O Tannenbaum." The model will be on display in the parish hall after the service.

3:30 p.m. Service of Praise and Thanksgiving

Greetings from . . . .

Mr. Roland Hennig, Chairman, 100th Anniversary Committee
Mr. Ivan Boles, Chairman, St. Matthew Lutheracn Church

Rev. Dr. Ed Lehman, President, Lutheran Church - Canada
Rev. Harold E. Ruf, President, Alberta British Columbia District
Rev. Dr. L. Dean Hempelmann, President, Concordia Seminary, Edmonton
Rev. Richard Kraemer, President, Concordia College, Edmonton
Rev. Dan Rinderknecht, Circuit Counselor, Stony Plain Circuit

Mr. Laurie Schutz, Lutheran Life Insurance Company

Hon. John Williams, Member of Parliament
Hon. Stan Woloshyn, Member of Legislature
Mayor Peter Marchiel, Stony Plain, Alberta
Mayor Joe Acker, Spruce Grove, Alberta
Reeve Peter Woloshyn, County of Parkland

Processional Banners

The processional banners for the One Hundredth Anniversary were designed by Linda Nowoczin and Tammy Parfieniuk.

Keynote Address by Pastor Carl Beiderwieden on the Anniversary Day

November 6, 1994 - Hebrew 2 parts of verses 1 and 2:

"We must pay more careful attention .... to what we have heard.......... for how shall we escape if we ignore such a great salvation? This salvation which was first announced by the Lord, was confirmed to us by those who heard Him." In the name of the Lord of the church, dear Christian friends:

When I received the invitation to be your guest speaker for this occasion, I wrote back that I was honored and excited at the prospect. Coming to St. Matthew and Stony Plain 68 years ago was one of the great adventures of my life. I remember so many details. Here I was confirmed. Here I was nurtured physically and spiritually through the formative years of my life. So I feel a close bond to this place and I was delighted to accept the invitation. However, I pointed out that this celebration was still a year and half away at that time and that I wasn't getting any younger or any healthier, so it was really a matter of "God willing if I should be here". Well here I am, so I suppose it is not presumptuous to say that God willed it. And St. Matthew is still here, and God willed that! And it has been here for 100 years, and God willed that too!

Not many congregations celebrate a 100th birthday. That makes this an historic event. In our hymns this morning we are praising God for His goodness and faithfulness; and in our prayers we thank Him for His grace and providence. But in our meditation we turn our attention for a few moments to history — the history of the church, the history of a congregation, and to your personal history. Some people mark history by its wars. They recall that this or that occurred during such and such a war. Some people mark history by eras — - they speak of the middle ages, the renaissance, the era of the Industrial Revolution, and the like. Others divide history by events, like Columbus's discovery of the new world, or man's first steps on the moon. But history is neither wars, nor eras, nor events. History is people. History is the story of people. Secular history is the story of peoples inhumanity towards other people, demonstrated in beatings, murders, and warfare. Secular history is the story of people in their greed walking over other people to achieve what they desire for themselves. Secular history is the story of lustful people striving to satisfy all the basic urges of the flesh. The secular history of this world is a story of evil and wickedness! Pick up any daily newspaper and you find its pages filled with accounts of murder and rape, of terrorism and vandalism, of adultery and fornication and sexual harassment, of thievery and fraud, protest and revolution, child and drug abuse and you are reading a microcopy of the secular history of mankind. Moses wrote: "the imagination of man's heart is evil from his youth."

Alongside of this you can read another history, the history of God's kingdom here in time, the history of the Christian church. This is the history of Divine grace and forgiveness, of the power which always tries and indeed can overcome and change the secular history of this world. This history, too, is the story of people. It is the story of people who are passing along a Word! Listen to the text: "This salvation which was first announced by the Lord, was confirmed to us by those who heard Him." See what happened? Jesus spoke a WORD. Those who were with Him heard it. They then spoke it to us (i.e. the author of this epistle and those who were with Him). Now we are writing it in this epistle so others may hear it! Passing on a WORD!

And what was that WORD? Our text says: "How shall we escape if we ignore such a great salvation" SALVATION! Not just any kind of salvation but such a GREAT salvation! This salvation announced by our Lord was GREAT in its origin. It sprang from the eternal love of the almighty creator God, and was so great that it encompassed all mankind. It was a love that determined to redeem His creatures from the Godlessness that they had chosen for themselves; to redeem them through a substitute whom God himself would provide through a woman's seed.

That salvation was GREAT in it's fulfilment. Although that Promised One came in all humility - the Christ child born of a lowly virgin - yet it was at once announced by angels from heaven that this was "Emmanuel", that is, "GOD with us!" God came in the flesh so that He might be placed under the Law and keep that Law in each and every respect. And having done so He took the burden of man's disobedience to that Law into His own heart and flesh and endured eternal punishment on the Cross. It was an agony unimaginable! Having endured it for each of us, he died — for that was the ultimate curse of our sin. By His resurrection He assured us of His vicarious victory. That's how this Great Salvation was accomplished.

But the real, abiding, joyous greatness of this salvation is to be found in it's RESULTS. "For God was in (this) Christ, reconciling the world unto Himself, not counting their sins against them!" Christ was not just the Lamb of God being offered up as some symbolic sacrifice — He was the Lamb of God "taking away the sin of the world!" Taking it away, so the Psalmist says: "as far as the East is from the West," "covering it" so that it can never again be found. In Christ, God met our one great need — for SIN which is our great problem, the cause of our fears, depressions, anxieties; the reason for death and its terrifying dread! All comes from sin. Our sin DAMNS! But Jesus now says: "Be of good cheer, your sins are FORGIVEN you": And because sin is forgiven He can promise: "I will come again and receive you unto myself, that where I am there you may be also!" You may retain all of the Scriptures, but if you throw away those passages which say: "the blood of Jesus Christ cleanses you from all sins" then you have nothing! On the other hand you can throw away all Scripture, but if you keep those passages which say: "the blood of Jesus Christ cleanses you from all sin" — then you have everything! This is the Word of the Great Salvation!

And this is the way that the visible church has been built — this is its history — passing that Word of the Great Salvation from parents to children, from generation to generation, from century to century. As each soul is made to lay hold on that Word another stone is added to the structure of the church. This is the only way that the church has been built, the only way that it can ever be built. We can have church-growth programs, and evangelism outreaches, and stewardship seminars — and they are all good in themselves — but if they do not have as their one objective the passing of the Word about the Great Salvation then they are useless. Only that Word builds the church.

What is true of the church as a whole is true of the parts. What is true of the whole Kingdom of God is true for the individual congregations which make up that kingdom. And that brings us to another history.

One hundred years ago some people came to this place to settle. At that time it was called "Hoffnungsau" I'm not sure what an "Au" is, perhaps a meadow? — but I'm sure most of us know what "Hoffnung" is. Hope! What a fitting name, for these settlers were looking for a place where their hopes for a good life, in which they could worship God according to the guiding of their conscience, could be fulfilled. They came from what at that time was referred to as the "old country", in contrast to this still "new" country where there were virgin forests and land which had seen no plow. Now that this country has become like a well used rug, worn threadbare in the middle by greed and frazzled on the outside by political conflict we no longer make that comparison. They were ordinary people, experienced mainly as farmers. They were ordinary people, experienced mainly as farmers. They applied for homesteads and built their first homes — for the most part of logs and with sod roofs. That first spring they cleared enough land to seed some grain and plant gardens. They carried on "mixed-farming sowing various crops of grain, having cows to provide them daily with fresh milk and allowing them to make their own butter and cheese. They raised pigs and each fall would slaughter a heifer and a pig and preserve the meat for the winter by smoking it, using brine, or canning it. They made a variety of delicious sausages. They raised chickens and ducks which provided eggs and a change of menu. They cultivated large vegetable gardens and preserved their produce in root cellars. They were for all practical purposes self contained in their livelihood. There was never an end to work in this kind of farming. It needed many hands — and God blessed them with large families. It was a day and a way of life when children were considered an economic asset and not a liability. They brought with them from the old country their own recipes and once you had tasted cabbage rolls and bratwurst in this area they never tasted the same again in any other place. They brought with them their customs and moral standards, many of which became a sturdy part of the Canadian culture.

But above all else and most precious of all they brought with them the Word of the Great Salvation! They wanted to keep that Word for themselves. They wanted to pass it on to their children. So they organized a congregation: actually a second congregation after some difficulties with the first. They called a pastor, Emil Eberhardt. He was just an ordinary person as were they, but he possessed several attributes that made him fitting for this place at that time. He, too, had the Word of the Great Salvation in Christ Jesus. He rightly divided that Word in its application to their lives. He proclaimed the law in its severity and the gospel with all of its sweet comfort of forgiveness. He also had a vision for the church. He knew that a single congregation standing by itself would have difficulty surviving. So he helped other groups of settlers in various locations throughout Alberta and British Columbia to organize congregations. He was most interested in the founding of the Alberta- British

Columbia District so that congregations could work together, and in the establishment of a college to help in the training of future pastors. And not least of all he had a strong will. Some called it stubbornness. I always thought of it to be determination. Once he determined the right way to go it was most difficult to change His mind. But his resolve saw him and the congregation through many a difficulty.

After the congregation was organized a place of worship was erected. It was part of a log parsonage. Later a real church was built in the architectural style eventually seen in churches all across the prairies. Still later another church was dedicated to the Lord, one of great beauty, made of stone, reminding the worshippers of the solid rock of the Word. Now the congregation worships in this recently erected structure.

The congregation also built a school, then two schools and finally consolidated them into one school. The purpose of all this building activity of church and schools was to pass the Word of the Great Salvation — from parent to children, from decade to decade, from generation to generation. And the congregation grew and prospered. She gave birth to daughter congregations and as her young people began to spread their wings they took their dedication to the Word wherever they settled.

And tomorrow? Well, that is really a third history. Your personal history! As the whole church has a history, and as each congregation which makes up that church has a similar history, so you who make up a congregation have a matching history. And your personal history is the most exciting of all.

Some years ago I drove past a museum which had a sign: "without the past there is no future". So also in our lives as the children of God. There is so much past history that has made each one of us a Christian today. Personally, for many of us, it started at the baptismal font. For some it was later in life that God made you his children. But no matter when the time in our lives might have been, some place in the past — long before your time or mine — a loving God permitted His Son to pay the price of our sin on Calvary's Cross. In that death there is forgiveness, and in Christ's resurrection there is eternal life. God called you to that blessed hope by creating saving faith in your heart. He has, since then, preserved your soul in that faith. That is part of your wondrous past history! Remember it! Nothing greater than that has ever happened to you! Nothing greater than that will ever happen to you! It started with God's love and Christ's sacrifice. God's love goes back to eternity and Christ's sacrifice goes back almost 2000 years. So God had to see to it that His church — His believing children — moved down

through the centuries to reach you. He had to see to it that the Word of the Great Salvation moved through years to sound in your ears. There had to be someone of God who brought you to be baptized, and who patiently taught you the meaning of your saving faith. That was most likely your parents. But for them to do that, someone had to bring them to be baptized, probably your grandparents. But for your grandparents to do that... you see we could go back through time and on and on. Indeed through the centuries there had to be hundreds and thousands like that or the Word of the Great Salvation would never have come to your time and to your heart. The whole history of all other Christians and thus the whole history of St. Matthew lies behind your being a Christian today. What a chain of people (there have been between Christ and You!) passing on the Word of Salvation! so many of them a part of the history of this congregation. And now you, each member of this congregation, are the last link in that chain, in this place and at this time. And you have the Word of that Great Salvation!

Will St. Matthew celebrate its 150 Anniversary in 2044? It all depends on you! And what YOU do with that Word! Amen.

Gottes Wort fur Ein Jahrhundert Johannes 17:14

Pastor Murvyn Kentel

Teure St. Matthaus Gemeinde:

Heute konnen wir als Glieder und Anwesende zu diesem Feiertag unsere herzen mit dem Psalmist erhaben und ertonen: "HERR GOTT, DU BIST UNSERE ZUFLUCHT FUR AND FUR." Denn heute preisen wir unsem Dreieinigen Gott dasz Er unsere Zuflucht fur ein Jahrhundert gewesen ist. Fur ein hundert jahren ist die Botschaft des Gekreuzigten Heilandes hier erschallt, und die Heilige Sacramente verwaltet und erhalten worden.

Mit freude gedenken wir an die Gnade und Gute unseres Barmherzigen Gottes. Wir danken Ihm mit herzen, mund und handen.

Das Wort Gottes worauf wir unsere betrachtung gegrundet haben errinert uns an die groszte Gabe Gottes wahrend diesem vergangendem Jahrhundrets: namlich Gottes Heiliges und Reines Wort. Jesus betet fur seine Junger, seine Kirche, ja die Gemeinde; "Vater, Ich habe ihnen dein Wort gegeben."

In gleicher weise betet Er heute zu seinem Himmeiishen Vater: "Vater, fur ein Jahrhundert habe ich der Matthaus Gemeinde dein Wort gegeben." Wie einst seine ersten Junger in einer kalten, bosen, sundhaftiger Welt lebten, so war es auch fur euch in dem vergangendem Jahrhundert gewesen. Gleich wie Gottes Wort den ersten Junger nutzlich war, also Trost und Hilfe in ihrem jammertai, so was das selbige Wort auch euch nutzlich also Hilfe und Beistand zu euerem leben und tun als eine Gemeinde Gottes.

"Ich habe ihnen dein Wort gegeben." Unser Heiland der seinen ersten Junger Gottes Wort gegeben hatte, seht auf die Matthaus Gemeinde, betet seinen Himmeiishen Vater an, spricht und sagt "Ich hab ihnen dein Wort gegeben."

Fur einhundert jahren hat die Matthaus Gemeinde das wahre, reine, von Gott eingegebende Wort geglaubt und erhaltet. Fur ein hundert jahren war dieses Gottes Wort der einzige grand euere Lehre und Leben. Fur ein hundert jahren haben die gleider bekannt "Himmel and Erde werde vergehen, aber Gottes Wort wird nie vergehen." Auf grand dieses Wort glauben ihr geliebte zuhorer und gestgenossen, dasz Gott der Schopfer Himmels and Erde ist; das der Dreieinige Gott der einzige und wahrer Gott ist, und aus Gottes Wort habt ihr gelemt und bis hierher glaubt ihr das Jesus Christus nicht nur wahrer Mensch ist, aber auch wahrer Gott ist, der eingebome Gottes Sohn, empfangen von dem Heiligen Geist, und von der Jungfrau Maria geboren. Weiter glaubt ihr das dieser Gott - Mensch sein schuldloszes Leben in den Tod fur euere Sunden gegeben hat, wie der Apostel Paulus erklart: "Er ist um unser Sunden willen dahingegeben, um unserer Gerechtigkeit willen auferweckt." Er hat euere Sunden schult bezahlt, nicht mit gold oder silber, sondem mit seinem unschuldigen Leiden and Sterben. Er hat euch mit Gott versohnet und eine ewige Wohnung im hause des Vaters bereitet.

Fur ein jahrhundert, hat der Heilige Geist dutch Wort und Sacrament euch in diesem wahren, selig machenden Glaube erhalten. Dutch das Wort des Gesetzes hat der Geist Gottes euch zur erkenntnisz euere Sunden gefuhrt, und dutch die frohe Botschaft des evangeliums Vergebung der Sunden versichert, denn das Blut Jesu Christi macht uns rein von alien Sunden. Fur ein hundert jahren hatte die Matthaus Gemeinde Friede mit Gott erlebt. Denn dieses Wort ist euere Starke in schwacheit, Trost in Trubsal, und Hoffnung in Verzweiflung gewesen. Es gibt nichts in dieser irdischen Welt dasz Mann mit Gottes Wort vergleichen kann, denn dieses wort welches Jesus der Heiland euch gegeben hat.

Fur die Zukunft geliebte, bittet und betet: "Gib uns femer dein teueres Wort. Heilige uns Herr in deiner Wahrheit, dein Wort ist die Wahrheit." Der segen Gottes fur ein Jahrhundert. Durch dasz, von Christo gegebende Wort hatte der Heilige Geist euere Christliche Gemeinde erbaut und zum werk des Amtes zugerichtet. Euer weiterfuhrendes Amt, euer Befehl und Auftrag als eine Christliche Gemeinde zu verkundigen, mit alien Menschen zu bescheren. Das Wort des Evangelium ist doch die kraft Gottes die da selig macht, alle die daran glauben. Das war doch euere aufforderung des ersten Jahrhunderts. Unzahlbare Menschen, verwandte und bekannte, wandelen doch noch in geistlicher finstemisz herum — Gottlos, Glaubenslos, Hoffnungslos. Es gibt keine andere Heilung fur die geistliche Krankheit die um uns liegt in dieser Sundhaftigen und bosen Welt, denn die frohe Botschaft des Wortes Gottes. Gott had dieses sein Wort unter euch fur ein Jahrhundert erschallen lassen. Gebet, bescheret, verkundiget dieses Seligmachende Wort von der Liebe Gottes in Christo zu jeder gelegenheit —— und beten mit dem dichten

Ach bleib bei uns Herr Jesus Christ,
Weil es nun Abend warden ist.
Dein Gottlich Wort, das Helle Licht,
Lasz ja bei uns ausloschen nicht.

Dein Wort ist unseres herzens Trutz,
Und deiner Kirche wahrer Schutz.
Dabei erhalt uns Heber Herr,
Dasz wir nichts naders suchen mehr

Gib dasz wir Leben in deinem Wort,
Und daraufferner fahren fort.
Von hinnen aus dem jammertai,
7M dir in deinem Himmelsaal. Amen.

God's Word for One Hundred Years (Translation)

St. John 17:14 Pastor Murvyn Kentel

Faithful members of St. Matthew

Today we can as members of St. Matthew and worshippers here, observe a celebration such as this one and declare with the Psalmist, "Lord God, thou art our refuge and strength forever more." For today we praise our Triune God for having been our help and refuge for the last one hundred years. For one hundred years the Gospel of our crucified Saviour has been preached and the Holy sacraments administered in all their purity. With joy we remember the grace and goodness of our merciful Father. We raise thanks to Him with our hearts, hands and voices.

The Word of God where upon we base our text, reminds us of the greatest of God's gifts that we received during the past one hundred years, namely God's pure and Holy Word. Jesus prayed for His disciples, for His Church, yes even for His congregation, "Father, I have given them your word".

In the same manner, He prays today to His Heavenly Father, "Father, for one hundred years, have I given St. Matthew congregation Thy Word".

Just as His first disciples lived in a cold, evil and sinful world, so it was for you in the past one hundred years. Just as the Word of God was a necessary tool for the early disciples in their world of sin, so the same Word was necessary as a help and assurance for living, and guiding you, as members of God's congregation.

"I have given them your Word". Our Saviour, who gave His first disciples God's Holy Word, looked down upon St Matthew congregation, prayed to His Heavenly Father and said, "I have given them your Word".

For one hundred years St. Matthew congregation believed the true, pure and inspired Word of God and kept it. For one hundred years this Word of God was the only reason for our Doctrine and Christian living. For one hundred years have the members of St. Matthew acknowledged that "Heaven and Earth will pass away, but God's Word shall never pass away". On the foundation of these words, you dear members and worshippers believe that God created Heaven and Earth; that the Triune God is the true and only God, and from the scriptures you have learned and believed that Jesus Christ was not only true man but also true God, the only Begotten Son of God, conceived by the Holy Spirit bom of the Virgin Mary. Further, you believe that this God-man laid down His sinless life into death as St. Paul has explained; "He willingly laid down His life for us and for our righteousness sake, arose again from the dead". He paid for our sins, not with gold and silver, but with His Holy precious blood, and His innocent suffering and death. He has made us righteous before God and provides for us a home in Heaven. For one hundred years the Holy Spirit has kept you through Word and Sacrament in Faith. Through the Word of the Law the Holy Spirit has shown you your sin and assured you through the Gospel that your sins are forgiven, for the Blood of Jesus Christ cleanses us from all sin.

For one hundred years St. Matthew congregation has enjoyed a Peace with God for all who believe it. For the Word of God is your power in weakness, a trust in distress, a hope in despair.

There is nothing in this world that can compare

with these words that Jesus the Saviour has given to you.

For the future dear members; ask and pray: "Give us your true Word and Truth." These are the Blessings of one hundred years.

Through Christ's promises, the Holy Spirit was able to build your congregation and equipped you to go forth. Your continuing efforts as a Christian congregation are clear; to preach the Gospel to all people and to share this Gospel with everyone, remembering that it is a power of God unto salvation to all those that believe it.

This was your responsibility for the first one hundred years. Countless people, friends and relatives, are still walking in Spiritual darkness, Godless, Faithless and Hopelessness. There is no other cure for the Spiritual sickness which is ail around us in this sin sick world, except the saving Gospel in God's Word.

God has permitted this Word to echo throughout the world. God has permitted this Gospel to be preached among you for one hundred years. Pray, provide and preach this Gospel of Salvation and God's love in Christ Jesus. The fields are ripe and the workers are few, so pray with every opportunity for God's Blessings.

With the song writer we rejoice,
Oh: *Stay with us Lord Jesus Christ,*

> *As the twilight fast approaches.*
>
> *Your Holy Word, your Holy light,*
>
> *May always guide us through the night.*
>
> > *Amen.*

Greetings from ...
Church

Roland Hennig
Anniversary Committee Chairman

Ivan Boles
Congregational Chairman

District and Synod

Rev. Dr. Ed Lehman
President Lutheran Church-Canada

Rev. Harold Ruf
President Alberta-British Columbia District

Rev. Dr. L. Dean Hempelmann
President Concordia Seminary, Edmonton

Rev. Richard Kraemer
President Concordia College, Edmonton

Greetings from ...
District and Synod

Rev. Dan Rinderknecht
Circuit Counselor, Stony Plain Circuit

A Fraternity of the Lutheran Church

Mr. Laurie Schutz
Lutheran Life Insurance Company
Representative

Greetings from ...
Government

Hon. John Williams, MP
Government of Canada, Ottawa

Hon. Stan Woloshyn, MLA
Government of Alberta, Edmonton

Mayor Peter Marchiel
Town of Stony Plain

Mayor Joe Acker
City of Spruce Grove

Reeve Peter Woloshyn
County of Parkland #70

Hon. Stan Woloshyn presenting a
plaque to Ivan Boles congregational
chairman

Following the Anniversory Service ...

Food and Fellowship

Setting the tables ...

Preparing the food ...

Serving the food ...

Enjoying the meal ...

History Remembered ...
Through Words, Picture ond Sound

Words and Pictures

Lights, Camera and Action

The Pastors' Messages

Pastor Eberhardt preaching from the Cairn marker on the occasion of the 25th Anniversary in 1919.

Pastor G. H. Raedeke conducting the 50th Anniversary Service at the Cairn, site of the first church, August 6, 1944.

We Preach Christ Crucified

1 Corinthians 1:23

One hundred years! What a great blessing from God! During this time, God has faithfully served and led our congregation. He has given us faith in the waters of baptism, fortified our faith through His Word, and strengthened our faith in Holy Communion.

Our message for the last one hundred years has been the same as that of St. Paul, "....We preach Christ crucified." These words have given encouragement, hope, comfort, and strength to all of us. This is the message we have carried into our community, province, country, and world. During the last century, we resolved to preach, teach, confess, and hear no other words than, "... We preach Christ crucified."

As we begin a new century, our message must remain the same! There will be those who encourage us to change our message, to stop talking about sin and God's forgiveness, and to conform to the world. They will promise us growth and success if we stop preaching Christ crucified.

However, there is no other message to hear or to speak. The message that has served us for one century will serve us during the next hundred years. The proclamation of Christ crucified is the power of God for salvation from sin's punishment, sin's power, sin's guilt, and sin's wages. This is God's good news for sinful people. No other message is as powerful or as important as, "...We preach Christ crucified." Therefore, this will be the focus of our congregation's ministry until Jesus returns to give us the crown of everlasting life.

As you read the history of St. Matthew Evangelical Lutheran Church of Stony Plain, Alberta, you will see how the message of "Christ crucified" was the driving force that moved this congregation forward in ministry. May God bless your reading, remembering, and rejoicing.

Rev. Roger M. Sedlmayr
Pastor

Rev. Roger M. Sedlmayr ...

A Biography

Roger Michael Sedlmayr was born on June 13, 1958 in Chicago, Illinois to Roger and Barbara (Aufmann) Sedlmayr.

He was baptized at St. Gregory Catholic Church in Chicago on July 20, 1958. Pastor Sedlmayr was confirmed on Palm Sunday, 1972, at Faith Lutheran Church of Tucson, Arizona.

Pastor Sedlmayr attended Faith Lutheran School of Tucson, Arizona from Grade One through Grade Five. He also attended Blenman and Wheeler Elementary Schools, Carson Jr. High School, and graduated from Palo Verde High School in 1976.

Pastor Sedlmayr attended Concordia Teacher's college at Seward, Nebraska from 1978 to 1982, graduating with a Bachelor of Science degree in Elementary Education. He then attended Concordia Seminary at St. Louis, Missouri from 1982 to 1986, graduating with a Master of Divinity degree.

On May 29, 1983, Pastor Sedlmayr and Joyce Wolters of Neepawa, Manitoba were joined together in marriage at St. John Lutheran Church of Seward, Nebraska. Their marriage has been blessed with three children: Niccole Michelle, bom February 14, 1985 in Storm Lake, Iowa; Danielle Elisse, bom March 17, 1987 in Dickinson, North Dakota; and Roger Matthew, born October 3, 1989 in Dickinson, North Dakota.

Pastor Sedlmayr has served as a summer intern at Family of Christ Lutheran Church at Andover, Minnesota (1980); and Fountain of Life Lutheran Church at Tucson, Arizona (1981 and 1982). He served a summer vicarage at Peace Lutheran Church of St. Louis, Missouri in 1983. His vicarage assignment was to Pilgrim and Trinity Lutheran Churches at Quimby and Marcus, Iowa (1984-1985). During his final year at the seminary, he served Grace Lutheran Church of De Soto, Missouri (1985-1986).

Pastor Sedlmayr was ordained into the Office of the Holy Ministry on the twenty eighth anniversary of his baptism, July 20, 1986. He served Redeemer Lutheran Church in Dickinson, North Dakota from 1986- 1992. He came to St. Matthew Lutheran Church in Stony Plain, Alberta in January of 1992 as associate pastor. He was appointed Senior Associate Pastor on April 24, 1994.

"Living Stones"

Our church has continued as a memorial to the saving grace of our Lord, Jesus Christ, for one hundred years. But the term "memorial" conjures up images of slain soldiers. Our memorial is different, however. It commemorates not one who is dead but one who lives and reigns to all eternity.

St. Matthew is more than a mere memorial. It is a living, active, and holy institution. The building is stone upon stone, but the church is made of "living stones, being built into a spiritual house to be a holy priesthood, offering spiritual sacrifices acceptable to God through Jesus Christ." (1 Peter 2:5)

The gracious blessings which have brought us to this day have a foundation far deeper than just one hundred years. Our solidarity is grounded in our common confession of faith expounded in the Book of Concord, 1580. Our heritage is "built on the foundation of the apostles and prophets, with Christ Jesus Himself as the chief cornerstone." (Eph. 2:20)

We mark days and years a celebrations of our faith together, but let us not forget the celebration that far outshines any event of the past. It is the continuing weekly celebration by which God graciously bestows on each of us a saving faith and the forgiveness of sins. Just as our God has lovingly acted in history for our sakes, so He continues to act just as profoundly each Sunday when His living Word and strengthening sacraments are freely given.

St. Matthew is built of "living stones" established on the solid rock of God's Word. If we continue to build on this foundation and we remain true to our cornerstone, Jesus Christ, one hundred years will be only the beginning.

William C. Heine, Associate Pastor
Advent, 1994

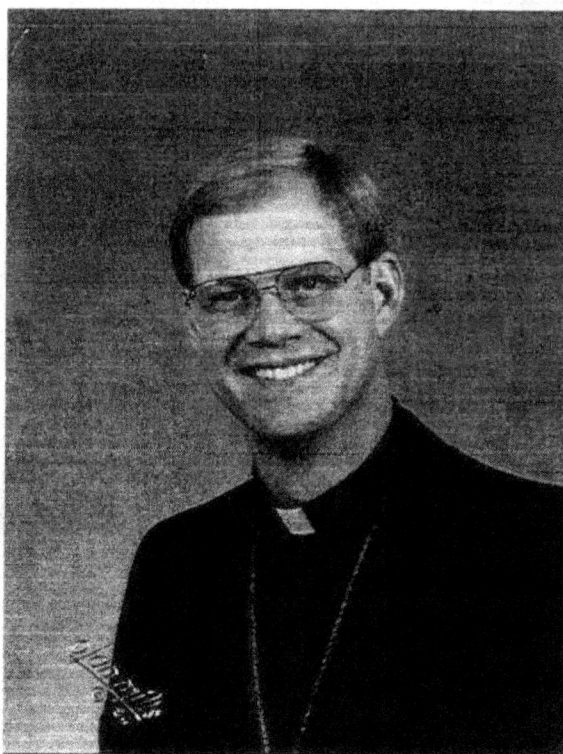

Rev. William C. Heine ... A Biography

Pastor William Charles Heine was born in Lexington, Nebraska to Gilbert and Aurelia (Ringenberg) Heine on May 3, 1954. He was made an heir of eternal life twenty days later through the washing of regeneration in the waters of Holy Baptism at Lexington's Trinity Lutheran Church on May 16,1954.

His elementary education began near Lexington in a one-room country schoolhouse and continued after grade four at St. John Lutheran School in Seward, Nebraska. He graduated in 1972 from Concordia High School in Seward, Nebraska. In 1978, he received his Bachelor of Science degree in Education and his Lutheran Teacher's Diploma from Concordia Teachers College also in Seward.

Following his college graduation, Mr. Heine taught in Lutheran elementary schools at St. Paul Lutheran School in Rockford, Illinois and at Trinity Lutheran School in Berrien Springs, Michigan. In the fall of 192, he entered Concordia Seminary in St. Louis, Missouri. He was awarded the Master of Divinity degree in May of 1986 and was ordained into the office of the Holy Ministry on June 29, 1986.

Pastor Heine served St. John Lutheran Church in Gregory, South Dakota, from 1986 to 1989. He accepted a call to Our Savior Lutheran Church in Pagosa Springs, Colorado, in 1989. In 1992 he helped found the Our Savior Lutheran School in Pagosa and served for two years as Headmaster of the school along with his pastoral duties. He continued as pastor at Our Savior until 1994. Pastor Heine was installed as associate pastor in St. Matthew Lutheran, Stony Plain, Alberta on October 2, 1994.

Pastor Heine is married to Melinda (nee: Smith). Melinda was born in Minneapolis, Minnesota. She grew up in Grinnell, Iowa and Cascade, Colorado. Melinda is a 1979 graduate of Concordia Teachers College in Seward, Nebraska. She taught at St. Paul Lutheran School in Rockford, Illinois before their children were born. She was the founding teacher of Our Savior Lutheran School in Pagosa Springs, Colorado in 1992. She was recognized by the Rocky Mountain District of the LCMS as "Teacher of the Year" in 1993.

The Heines have four children: Katherine (1980), Sarah (1985), Karl (1986), and Susan (1988).

Dear Members and Friends of St. Matthew Lutheran Church

One hundred years! That certainly seems like a long time! After all, no one who was around then is still alive. If we reckon a generation as twenty-five years, then St. Matthew congregation has seen four generations of members.

We have come from all walks of life, from all parts of Canada and the world. Most of the original members were settlers who came from Germany and parts of Ukraine. These original members were faithfully ministered to by Dr. Eberhardt, a pastor whose commitment to the Gospel led him to do mission work in other parts of Alberta and British Columbia. Under the leadership of Pastor Eberhardt and through the working of the Gospel, St. Matthew Church developed as a congregation that was and still is very supportive of mission work.

Present day members consist of long-time residents of the community and newcomers from all parts of Canada and the United States. We all share one thing: we have been blessed through Word and Sacrament ministry and confess the faith of our Living Saviour.

We share that faith in Jesus even with those who have long since left this life and now belong to the Church Triumphant in heaven. That is certainly a testimony to the power of the Gospel and to the incomparable grace of God in His Son.

This 100th anniversary is an occasion to rejoice and give thanks for what God has done. It is also a time to re-consecrate ourselves to our confession of faith and to the mission our Lord has given us. As Christ's church, we are to carry that saving message in ministry to one another and in outreach to those who do not know the Living Lord. There is only one way to carry out that mission. We need to continue to "... preach Christ and Him crucified."

The first year of a marriage usually sets the tone for the rest of the marriage. It is my prayer that the first century of St. Matthew's history is indicative of what is yet to come under God's blessing.

Rejoicing in His days, Donald R.

Schiemann
Rev. Donald Schiemann ... A Biography

Pastor Schiemann was born September 1, 1951 in Montreal, Quebec. He was baptized at Redeemer Lutheran Church in 1951 and confirmed there also in 1965. With his family, he moved to Cobourg, Ontario in 1967. He graduated from Cobourg District Collegiate Institute West in 1969. He then attended the University of Waterloo in Waterloo, Ontario. He graduated in 1972 with a B.A. and enrolled at Concordia Theological Seminary in Springfield, Illinois to begin his studies for the holy ministry. He vicared at St. Paul's Lutheran Church in Kitchener, Ontario. He graduated from the seminary in 1976 with a Master of Divinity degree, majoring in exegetical theology.

Pastor Schiemann was called by the Ontario District to serve as a Missionary- at-Large in Corunna, Ontario. He was ordained in May of 1976 at Holy Cross Lutheran Church, Kitchener, Ontario. On July 3, 1976, Pastor Schiemann married Beth Israel. In October of 1977, Pastor Schiemann was called as pastor to the newly-formed Ascension Lutheran Church in Corunna, Ontario. The mission congregation continued to grow and in 1981 built a chapel. During their time in Corunna, the Schiemanns were blessed with three children: Michael (born 1977), Peter (born 1979) and Julia (born 1981). Pastor Schiemann continued to serve in Corunna until 1984 when he accepted a call to Good Shepherd Lutheran Church in London, Ontario. In 1988, he accepted a Call to St. Matthew Lutheran Church in Stony Plain, Alberta. Pastor Schiemann served there until 1994 when he accepted a Call to serve as Executive Assistant - Mission Services for the Alberta-British Columbia District.

During the Anniversary planning stages, Pastor Schiemann was pastor at St. Matthew. At the time of publication of this book, Pastor Schiemann had accepted a call extended by the Alberta-British Columbia District to serve as Executive Assistant-Mission Services. We regret his leaving, but wish him God's richest blessing in his new endeavors.

Danket dem Herrn

"Danket dem herm, denn er ist freundlich, und seine guete wehret ewiglich," (Ps. 118, 1). Dies Wort des Psalmisten ist auch unser Wahlspruch bei dieser Jubelfeier. Mit Herzen, Mund and Haenden danken wir Gott dem Herm, der so freundlich, gnaedig und barmherzig ist. Seine Guete und Treue ist alle Morgen neu. Er hat uns reichlich gesegnet und hat alle seine Verheissungen wahr gemacht.

Das hat Gott getan nicht weil wir es verdient haben, sondem weil er so guetig und freundlich ist, und weil unser Heiland fuer uns gestorben und auferstanden ist. Weil der Heiland fuer uns die Suendenschuld bezahlt hat durch sein Leiden und Sterben, handelt Gott mit uns nicht nach Verdienst, sondem mit Gnade und Barmherzigkeit. Damm danken wir dem Herm and preisen seinen heiligen Namen.

Diese Guete und Barmherzigkeit Gottes nimmt kein Ende. Sie wehret ewiglich. Was Gott verspricht das haellt Er auch. Gottes Wort ist wahrhaftig. Auf Gottes Wort und Verheissung koennen wir uns verlassen. Darum koennen wir also seine lieben Kinder und als Glieder seiner Kirche und Gemeinde getrost und gutes Muths auch femerhin Gottes Reich bauen. Dazu sind wir berufen. Das ist unsere Aufgabe. Moege der Gott aller Gnade, der freundlich ist und dessen Guete ewiglich wehret, das Werk der St. Matthaeus gemeinde auch in der Zukunft reichlich segnen Ihm zur Ehre von Ewigkeit zu Ewigkeit.

L. H. Gierach April, 1993

Thank the Lord

(Translation from German) *by Jack C. Schram*

"Oh, give thanks unto the Lord; for He is good; because His mercy endureth forever." (Ps. 118:1) These words of the Psalmist, are also the words chosen for our thoughts on this our 100th anniversary. With hearts and hands and voices, we thank our God for His endless Grace and Mercy which is new to us every morning. He has richly blessed us, and made every promise come true. He has done all that not because we have earned it, but because of his Grace and Mercy through the death and resurrection of His only begotten son, Jesus Christ, who has borne our sins through his suffering and death on the cross. Because of His extended Grace and Mercy, God the Father can now deal with us not because we have earned it, but because of His extended Grace and Mercy through His only begotten son Jesus Christ. For all this, we thank and praise His Holy Name.

The Grace and Mercy of God has no end and lasts forever. What God promises He helps, and His word is forever true. On His word and promises we can rely. Therefore we can be his dear children, and as members together we can move forward in building His Kingdom, for which we are called to do. May the God of Grace, Mercy and Goodness bless the work of St. Matthew congregation to move forward in the future to his Glory now and forever more and into all eternity.

Recollections and Reflections *by Rev. Lester H. Gierach*

My first contact with St Matthew Lutheran Church was in early August, 1946 when I was on my way to be ordained and installed in my first parish — the Hines Creek Parish at the end of the railroad in northern Alberta. The event was a farewell gathering for Teacher Philip Enders, who had accepted a call to another school. The Hines Creek Parish, at that time, consisted of five stations; St. Paul's congregation (nine miles south of Hines Creek); St. Peter's congregation, ten miles north of Hines Creek; Trinity congregation in Fairview, and preaching stations in Berwyn and Peace River. In the Hines Creek congregations I conducted services in German on a regular basis. The fact that I had learned German at home as a child near Milwaukee, Wisconsin and expressed the willingness to use it regularly, no doubt influenced the Board of Assignments and the St. Louis Seminary to assign me to my first parish where regular German services were required. I thank the Lord for His guidance and direction, and for permitting me to stay and serve Him in western Canada ever since. The present church building in Fairview, Alberta was under construction when I accepted the call to Hope Congregation in Victoria, B.C.

In Victoria, I did not have the opportunity to preach German. When the call came to Zion, Surrey, Immanuel, and Aldergrove, B.C., I accepted it and conducted services in the German language on a weekly basis during my ministry there. During my years in Zion, Surrey, I always looked to St. Matthew in Stony Plain as an inspiration and model, especially in their efforts to maintain and expand the parochial school. I thank the Lord that I was privileged to be a part of Zion congregation in Surrey when they built and established Zion Lutheran School. It was opened in September, 1959 with 17 pupils in grades 1-4. The Lord has blessed Zion School beyond measure, and many blessings have come to Zion congregation as a result of the school.

After almost sixteen years of joyous service in Zion, Surrey, I came to Edmonton to serve as full-time Executive Secretary of the Alberta-British Columbia District. My responsibilities were for all areas of church work including missions, education, stewardship, evangelism, youth, church extension, etc. One of my first assignments from the District Board of Directors was to meet with St. Matthew Board of Education. St. Matthew School was in a little financial difficulty and had requested some funds from the district. I was asked to assess the situation and make a recommendation. I recommended that some funds be granted, and the District Board of Directors accepted the recommendation and granted some funds to "bail out" the school. Over the years it was my privilege to assist the congregation in various financial programs, and the Lord granted visible results.

My involvement at St. Matthew

was not exclusively related to finances. Over the years I have been privileged to conduct services on various occasions and, at times, rather regularly. One year during Pastor Gehring's hospitalization, I conducted all the Lenten Services - German and English on the same evening. I recall one Mission Festival also. It was held outside when a rainstorm interfered with the proclamation of my Mission message, and I had to cut the sermon short because the worshippers fled for cover to their cars, and my congregation disintegrated before my very eyes. I never did get to preach that entire sermon — yet. During the last few years I conducted German services twice a month on Sunday afternoons until they were discontinued in early 1993. The last regular German service was held on February 28, 1993. I am grateful to the Lord of the Church for the privilege to be involved over the years at St. Matthew congregation, and pray that the Lord will continue to bless His people at St. Matthew as they march forward and continue to do great things for His glory.

L.H. Gierach
April, 1993

Rev. Lester H. Gierach

My Association With St. Matthew, Stony Plain

My association with St. Matthew Lutheran Church dates back quite a number of years, perhaps not a century, but at least three quarters of a century. My parents, Johann Philip (known mostly as J.P.) Baron and Wilhelmina (Rauhland), came to Canada in 1898. They emigrated from Austria-Hungary, and came to Winnipeg, and to this part of the country three years later. My folks were members of St. Matthew either before, or at the time of, Pastor Reinitz's pastorate.

It was during the teaching term of J. Dobring that I started school. We moved to Stony Plain in 1917, and I remember not only the town school, but also walking to St. Matthew School in the country for Saturday school.

During my years at Concordia College, (I started in 1922) I, like so many of the students, came out to Stony quite often. One such occasion was when three of us drove back a team of horses from the college. After the new college was built, the grounds were in rough shape. The good people from Stony Plain, Leduc, and other places, were willing to loan their horses for a week, providing the students would work them, and bring them back. We must have started out between five and six o'clock. It was a chilly, more than twenty mile drive to the church in the country, where we were to leave the team. We decided to go to church, and promptly fell asleep, but we didn't sleep too long after Dr. Eberhardt started his sermon!

On another occasion, perhaps ten years later, I "reffed" a hockey game between the Outlaws and a team from the Journal. Needless to say at the end of the game I was as popular with both teams as any referee ever was.

One of the first pastoral conferences I attended as pastor was held in Stony. Pastor John Ohlinger and I stayed at the home of John Schram. Thank you, Mr. Jack. We had a pleasant stay with your folks.

Shortly after my wife and I were married, I preached at the mission festival "under the trees". We stayed at the Eberhardt residence and had the top floor to ourselves. Someone suggested that we should have brought our bikes, so we "could find each other".

Then came a day which I am sure many people of St. Matthew still remember. It was November 26, 1972, when I had my farewell services in the Whitecourt-Rochfort Bridge parish. Some time before, when talking with Pastor Gehring, we discussed the prospect of being neighbours again, since he was at Stony, and I would be going to Golden Spike. He had suggested that there might be times when we could help each other out, as we had done before. On that same Sunday, November 26, 1972, the Lord called Pastor Gehring to his heavenly home, while he was conducting a service. Neither of us had the slightest notion that by December 10, or two weeks later I would be conducting the service in German in Pastor Gehring's place. "Der Mensch denkt, aber Gott lenkt".

From then on, I conducted the services in German more or less regularly. This by the way was also the time, October 14,1973, when we began to hold services, in a rented Roman Catholic Hall, in Devon.

I retired as of December 31,1976, but continued to serve the parish until Pastor Morgret was installed, September 17, 1978. On November 26 of that same year, I had a note that Pastor Schoepp was to have heart surgery, so I was asked to take the service, the German as well as the communion services at St. Matthew.

This arrangement was interrupted somewhat by the fact that our congregation at Medicine Hat asked me to serve them during the vacancy. They had already been vacant for two years — mostly because they were unable to get a man who could handle the German. We did this on a "three weeks in and one week out basis" from the end of March to the end of July, when Pastor Gary Knoemschildt was installed there as a pastor. I carried on at St. Matthew in September, continuing quite regularly with the German services during 1980, and helping out at Lake Isle.

At the beginning of 1981,1 was asked by the Mission Board of the District to take the vacancy at Manville, and at the same time to "canvass" Vermilion for prospects. I agreed to do this with the provision that if there were sufficient prospects at Vermilion, services would be held. Consequently, Mrs. Baron and I left on Monday, February 23. We made calls all week inviting people, who either had some affiliation with the Lutheran Church, or who had no church home, to come to the service the following Sunday, March 1. We had made arrangements with Roger and Rose Gabert (since we knew Roger from Bethany, Beaver Hills from years before) to have services at their house. The Lord blessed our efforts and especially the prayers of His people. On March 1,1981 the first service of the Lutheran Church-Missouri Synod was held in Vermilion with 13 people in attendance. We also had confirmation instruction and a service at Manville that day, and then went home, to continue the work in German. We went back to Vermilion-Manville every month for a week, to make more calls, and then to hold services on Sundays until July 25, when Candidate Terry Richardson was installed there as pastor. The attendance at the installation service was 160. At Vermilion the attendance was up to 35.

The work load for me at St. Matthew was heaviest perhaps from the time that Pastor Murv Kentel was called and his installation on November 8, 1981.

I continued until 1986, when for several months we were asked to take over Manville-Vermilion once more, but continued with services in German into 1988. In January of 1988 we began the work of serving the vacancy at Fort McMurray, which lasted for about ten months. This meant that someone else had to carry on with the German services at St. Matthew on a regular basis.

However, I had the pleasure of taking part in the ground-breaking services at St. Matthew on April 3,1989.

In September of 1989 our family went to St. Catharines, Ontario where I was awarded the "Veteran of the Cross" by our Seminary. The nomination had come from a former member of St. Matthew.

On June 3,1990 came the dedication of Bethany Lutheran Church at Beaver Hills. It was my privilege to preach the sermon in the morning service. My ministry in this congregation had covered a period of thirteen years.

A similar event occurred on June 17 of the same year, when the new building of St. Matthew Lutheran was dedicated. I had the privilege of taking part in the dedication services here, and doing it in the German language.

My wife and I continue our membership in St. Matthew, usually attending the early morning service, or quite often attending worship service in a neighboring congregation. Services in German have been discontinued since the spring of 1993.

My long association with St. Matthew continues — perhaps not as actively as at former times — but it is my prayer that our Lord will continue to bless this congregation in the future as He has in the past.

To Him alone be the glory!
C.R. Baron, Pastor

AuxiliorY Organizations

Ladies Aid

Sunday School

Altar Guild

        Women's Missionary League

Senior Bible Class

Mom's Morning Out

Stephen Ministry

Ladies Aid Past and Present

The ladies meet monthly in the Parish Hall on the first Thursday of the month. The meetings start at 1:30 p.m. with a brief devotion, consisting of hymns, Scripture readings and prayer. Topical discussions were conducted at each meeting. One of the projects of the Ladies Aid was to gather "Portals of Prayer" devotion books, which were sent to Africa.

St. Matthew Ladies Aid received a "Certificate of Appreciation Award" from Concordia Lutheran Seminary from President W. Janzow in 1985.

Between 1987 and 1992, a large number of quilts and blankets were made. The blankets were sent to Ronald McDonald House, and the quilts to L.A.M.P. at High Level and Rainbow Lake. Three hundred and eight boxes of clothing were also sent.

Since 1982, contributions by the Ladies Aid to various charitable organizations included $3,362.00. In the last 10 years, the members of St. Matthew Ladies Aid made 1,982 visits to the Good Samaritan Nursing Home. They also visited with 386 members of the congregation. There were 1,749 calls and visits to Whispering Waters Manor and 135 hospital visits.

Theresia Goebel Secretary

The Ladies Aid of 1944

Figure 1Our Ladies Aid pictured here in January, 1995

St. Matthew Lutheran Sunday School

St. Matthew Lutheran Sunday School is a part of our church that has been, and still is, crucial to the spiritual growth of our children. Jesus said in Matthew, "Let the children come to me, and do not stop them, because the Kingdom of heaven belongs to such as these." In our world, opportunities are few to learn about the love of the Saviour, and Sunday School offers just that. It is a time to hear about Jesus and how He has saved us. It is a time for Bible stories, learning to pray and asking questions. Finally it is a time for singing, learning to share the good news and spending time with other Christians. Children in the past and in the present have enjoyed their time in Sunday School. It is our prayer that this tradition of good Christian Education will carry on into future generations.

Our Sunday School began in 1942. Pastor Gilbert Raedeke opened our Sunday School and taught until 1946. In 1953, Inga Church joined our congregation and our Sunday School grew. It was also in 1953 that Mrs. Clara Evjen began teaching and did so for 20 years. Mrs. Evjen saw many things which were important in the history of St. Matthew Lutheran Sunday School. Following are some of her reflections.

"In the year 1953, our little church at Inga was closed and we joined St. Matthew in Stony Plain.

I offered my services to teach Sunday School. It was at the time when Anna Miller and Margaret Schwed were leaders in the Sunday School. I always attended the Sunday School teacher's meetings. I taught the grade 5/6 class and had a nice group of children.

I remember one funny incident that happened during one lesson close to Christmas. The children were passing a paper to one another and I said, "Hey, give me that paper." I read that they were planning to buy me a Christmas gift. Needless to say, I didn't get a Christmas present that year. But most of the time, they were quite well behaved and enjoyed the lessons.

I thank God for giving me the privilege to serve as Sunday School teacher for 20 years.
Sincerely, Clara Evjen"

Presently, our Sunday School is blessed with a double teaching staff. We call it "team teaching". This has been very successful. Our teachers have worked out a schedule that makes sure that at all times children can remain in a class with their own teachers. Our attendance has reached a high of 60 children. We have a special class for preteens and teens. The grade 6-7 and 8 classes have each had a steady attendance of 6 but fluctuate to as many as 12! We have had many special Sundays. We hold "Fruit of the Spirit Sundays." These help the children recognize and understand gifts they receive from the Holy Spirit, such as patience, love, joy and self-control. We have had two craft Sundays and have had the chance to pass the love of Christ, on by singing to the people at the Good Samaritan Care Centre. The parents of our Sunday School have been very supportive and we appreciate that. I would also like to mention that recently we have been blessed with two song leaders, Mr. and Mrs. Clair Denninger. They have taken on the duty of having a 15 minute opening with the children every Sunday morning. So you see, the Lord is working in our Sunday School and we praise Him!

As teachers we are looking forward to 1994 and future years. We have been given the talent of teaching by Jesus Christ and we intend to use it. We would like to ask one thing of all of you that have just read about St. Matthew Sunday School past, present and future: PLEASE PRAY FOR US.
In His Service,
Laura Rockney

Research done by: Mrs. Alice Altheim, History written by: Mrs. Clara Evjen Written and Compiled by: Laura Rockney

Altar Guild Report

(Founded in 1947)

Altar Guild meets the 3rd Tuesday of the month 9 times per year. The meetings open with devotion and prayer. We strive to have interesting church related topics, at each of our meetings. Topic leaders are our pastors, teachers, lay people on occasion and some informative outside visitors.

We serve the Lord in many ways. Our first and foremost purpose is caring for and cleaning altar vestments, sanctuary items, communion ware and also purchasing altar vestments. We try to supply flowers for the sanctuary from our gardens in summer, and Easter lilies and poinsettias at the appropriate seasons.

Our commitment also includes looking after banners and confirmation gowns. We decorate the Christmas tree and supply lights and decorations as needed.

Annual events are the Birthday Party at the Meridian Foundation, Tea and Bake Sale, and a potluck Christmas party for our Altar Guild members and their spouses or friends.

Altar Guild makes regular donations to Concordia College Guild and Lutheran Hour Sponsor Plan. Other donations have been made to Lutheran Bible Translators (LBT)—Krenzke Mission, Lutheran Association of Missionaries and Pilots (LAMP), Rehoboth Christian Association and the cost of new kneelers.

The ladies of the Guild enjoy helping our church in every way possible including purchasing drapes, hymnals, kitchen items, flower stands and plants for the grounds. We also give of ourselves by serving at potluck suppers, workshops, funerals, installations, for senior functions and many other events.

A special project was spearheading the production of St. Matthew 90th Anniversary Cookbook in 1984. The Guild also supports various memorial projects.

God has blessed the Altar Guild and St. Matthew. We give praise and thanks to Him for our 100 year history!

Submitted by
Ethel Fielhaber

History of the St. Matthew Lutheran Women's Missionary League 1984 - 1994

The motto of the Lutheran Women's Missionary League (LWML) is "Serve the Lord With Gladness" and over the last ten years the Stony Plain society has been faithfully meeting that challenge. Along with collecting mites and donating resources and time to the various local, district, and international projects, the society has had some historical changes. With the forming of Lutheran Church- Canada in 1988, our society underwent a constitutional review, with several changes being adopted. "Article 1 - Name: The name of this society shall be St Matthew Lutheran Women's Missionary League at Stony Plain of the A-BC District of Lutheran Church-Canada", was one of the changes that was adopted in November of 1990.

Our society has continued to help various organizations, such as Concordia College, Concordia Lutheran Seminary, Women In Need (WIN) House, Hope Mission, Lutheran Institutional Ministry Edmonton (LIME), Lutheran Bible Translators (LBT) and Canadian Lutheran World Relief (CLWR). We have collected kits for the various in-gatherings for the District and International Conventions. Our society also aided the Grande Cache society in building a shelter for the mine workers in 1989. We arranged, through the Gideons, to have Bibles placed in the Stony Plain Hospital rooms. Since 1992, we have made a trip in the early spring to Hope Mission in the inner city, taking clothing, groceries and Christian reading material, preparing and serving an evening luncheon and leading the chapel service. Helping these many organizations keeps us
mindful of our many blessings and our mission statement.

Conventions are another important aspect of the LWML and the St. Matthew society has always provided for one or two delegates to attend. District and International Conventions gather many faithful women together to make decisions concerning the League and its work, especially the choosing of projects and the allocation of the mite monies to these projects. Significantly, the 75th Anniversary of the International LWML was celebrated in Cleveland, Ohio in 1991. The theme was "Celebrate the Jubilee! Glorify His Name!" What a celebration our delegates experienced with the indoor fireworks, the adoption of a $1,111,000 mission goal, and much singing and praising to our Lord.

Another event also occurred in Cleveland. Edmonton made a bid to host the next convention in 1993 and it was accepted. The years 1992 and 1993 were very busy for our Convention Host Committee, as well as all the societies in and around Edmonton. Many members of the St. Matthew society were on the host committee and many others served as volunteers before and during the convention. In the year 1993, the LWML in Canada officially left its sister organization in the United States and became its own organization, known as LWML-Canada. The International Convention was held June 17 - 20 with the Founding Convention following immediately on June 20 and 21.

With the birth of LWML-Canada, the Stony Plain society heads into 1994, busily planning for the 100th anniversary of the congregation, and lending a hand in the many activities being planned.

Respectfully Submitted, Becky Wandio Secretary 1990 - 1994

73

Pictured here are the members of the Women's Missionary League of 1994.

St. Matthew Lutheran Women's League Christmas Party December 16, 1992

Certificate of Membership

This is to Certify that _the Lutheran Woman's Missionary Society_

of _St. Matthew's Lutheran_ Church, located at

Stony Plain _Alberta Canada_

   City   State

is hereby received into membership with the

Lutheran Women's Missionary League

of

The Lutheran Church—Missouri Synod

District _Alberta British Columbia_   _Mrs. Rudolph Henry_
       Columbia   President

Date _November 9, 1958_   _Mrs. A. R. Siegh_
   Joined district 1954   Recording Secretary

Senior Bible Class

The Bible classes were started in December of 1979, when the Director of Christian Education at St. Matthew was Ken Olson. They were held twice a month on Wednesday mornings, except for July and August, and lasted an hour. We've had a membership of as high as 28 with an average attendance of 18 over the last 12 years.

Pastors and others that taught us were: Rev. W. Schoepp, Rev. M. Kentel, Rev. H. Witte, Rev. D. Schiemann, Rev. C. Baron, Rev. R. Sedlmayr, D.C.E. Ken Olson, Vicars Dan Hansard, Jim Schnaar and Jack Stoop; Ruth Adam, Carol Mohr, Judy Schutz and Carl Schutz.

All sessions were started with prayer and/or a caring session and closed with prayer and/or the benediction.

For many years, under the coordination of Ruth Adam and later Debbie Stresman of the fellowship club, the young women of the congregation served lunch to all the seniors of the congregation. These were later cut down to once a month and then discontinued. In 1988, Evelyn Hohnstein and Elizabeth Goertz served us lunch once a month from January to May. We want to take the opportunity to thank all of the women who served us the lovely lunches. We enjoyed the fellowship too.

In 1983 and 1984, some of the seniors went to the Lynnwood Nursing Home where Rev. Kentel had his German devotion and sing-song. We enjoyed helping with the singing and visiting with the patients.

Our monthly offerings were sent to Lutheran Bible Translators (LBT), Concordia College, Dr. Schwermann Scholarship Fund for seminary students, and the new church. In 1990, we voted to discontinue the offering and used the account of $1,070 to pay for 8 offering plates and the rail for the wheel chair ramp in memory of some of our members who had passed away.

Our Bible study group studied the following: The Congregational Cottage Meeting Studies, Jonah, I and II Peter, I,II and III John, I and II Samuel, Galatians, Luther's Small Catechism, Jude, Women of the Bible including videos by Dr. Kenneth E. Bailey, James, Job, Acts, Ruth, Daniel, Genesis and the Christmas Story from Luke and Matthew. Other topics were: Homosexuality, Together in Ministry, Churches in Russia, Social Ministry and Canadian Lutheran World Relief (CLWR).

We, the seniors, have been very blessed to have dedicated pastors and others who bring us the doctrinal truths of the Bible, to help us grow in our spiritual life. We thank God and each of you.

I would like to acknowledge the help I received from reports of Lillian Berndt and Emelia P. Hennig.

Elsie M. Kulak, Secretary

In this photograph we see the members of the Senior Bible Class.
The picture was taken on March 18,1992.

Mom's Morning Out

In the Spring of 1984, St. Matthew Lutheran Church was celebrating its 90th Anniversary. As part of the celebrations, a Fellowship Committee was formed. The purpose of this committee was to reach members of the congregation who were not being reached through the existing programs. One of the groups targeted for fellowship was mothers of preschool children. This was the beginning of St. Matthew's Young Mom's Group. Pastor Harold Witte strongly supported this idea and was instrumental in getting the group started.

Originally, the group was developed to provide a time of fellowship and a break for young mothers in the congregation. These objectives were to be reached through a program of Bible study and craft activities. The first Executive of the group was comprised of Liz Ryan, Joyce Berezan and Jean Kupsch.

The group made arrangements with St. Matthew School to use the kitchen as a meeting place and a spare room for a child-care area. Volunteer babysitters were booked through the congregation and pre-registration was held. In September of 1984, the first meeting of St. Matthew Young Mom's Group was held with an enrolment of 6 mothers.

The group faced many obstacles through its early years. Volunteer babysitters were always difficult to find so the group was forced to look outside of the church membership. It was decided that the babysitters should be paid an honorarium so a small fee was charged to the mothers using the service. It is only in the past few years that we have been blessed with reliable, caring women as babysitters for our children. We are very thankful for the service that Debbie Robin, Bernice Halliday, Dorothy Framingham and Pat Ulmer have provided for our children.

Originally, the group decided to meet on Wednesday mornings. One year this posed a problem for the school and meetings were changed to Wednesday afternoons. In another instance there was no available time at the school and meetings were held Wednesday mornings at the home of Kathy Patera. It is only because of the dedication and persistence of these mothers that the group continued to meet through adverse circumstances and continued to grow.

As administration at St. Matthew School changed, more support was shown for the Young Mom's Group. This group was recognized as the precursor to the Parent Teacher League (PTL) group and was highly supported. Gymnasium time was allotted to the group to provide space for their children and the mothers again met in the school kitchen.

In 1992, the group decided to change the name of the group to Mom's Morning Out. Crafts were dropped from the agenda and more of a focus was put on the Bible study time.

The group has grown in size considerably with an average weekly attendance of 12 mothers. The support these women have given to each other has been tremendous. In these changing times when the nucleus family of mothers, aunts, and grandmothers is not always close by to ask for assistance or just to talk to, the members of St. Matthew Mom's Morning Out group have been a life-line for one another. All this has been done in the name of Jesus Christ, as a witness to our faith and in loving service for one another.

Many ladies have been involved in the past 10 years of the group and all of the them should be given credit for the success of the group. Especially important were the following women who served as President of the St. Matthew Mom's Morning Out: Connie Pedersen, Mary Corson, Naomi Heselton, Kathy Patera, Laurie Parkinson, Heather Schoepp, Joyce Berezan and Liz Ryan.

However, it is by the grace of God and according to His will, that this group has grown and ministered to so many women and we thank Him for all of His blessings to us as mothers.

Submitted in His Name, Liz Ryan

Stephen Ministry

In 1986, Pastor Harold Witte initiated the Stephen Ministry Series

Program at St. Matthew. He approached Bob Enders to take the Leadership Training Course. In April of 1986, Bob went to Baltimore, Maryland to take part in the training. That fall the first lay members of our congregation began their Stephen Ministry training. They included: Ted and Mary Schuman Barb Enders Ethel Fielhaber Sandie Schutz Dean Litzenberger Elly van den Brande Our first class of Stephen Ministers was commissioned on March 15, 1987.

The second class of Stephen Ministers began its training in September of 1988. They included: Marvin Hennig Mildred Ulmer Russ Bardak Naomi Heselton Bev Rosnau Sharon Kloeck Lloyd Howlett Judy Schutz The second class of lay caregivers was commissioned on May 28, 1989.

At this time a request was made for a second leader. Lloyd Howlett expressed an interest in the leadership training and went to Los Angeles in June of 1989. After training, Lloyd proceeded to train our third class, beginning in September of 1989. His first trainees included:
Lawrence Hay Evelyn Litzenberger Judy Swanson Vicki Laramee Eleanor Unterschultz Dorothy Altheim Connie Pedersen This class was commissioned on May 6, 1990.

Our fourth class commenced training in October of 1991. The members of this class were: Lorraine Lutz Hilda Schoepp Minnie Schuttler These lay ministers were commissioned on June 28, 1992.

Our fifth class commenced training in October of 1992 and included: Trudy Walraven Ruth Adam Doreen Dewald Bernice Hennig They were commissioned on May 30, 1993.

When the program first began in 1986, our congregation was a little skeptical about accepting the help of our trained lay ministers. However, after a few months and a few successful ministries, we were accepted as a valuable helping resource. Today, our services are being utilized both inside and outside our congregation, to the point that we desperately need more trained Stephen Ministers.

Submitted by Lloyd Howlett, Stephen Leader

Participants of Stephen Ministry in 1994

Choirs

Senior Choir

Bill Quast directed the Senior Choir for ten years from 1978 to 1988. In addition to singing twice a month at regular services, the choir has performed at numerous concerts such as the Good Friday concert in 1987, a light hearted Valentine Revue, several year end concerts, Christmas celebrations involving choir, recorders and Orff instruments and enhancing installation services and other important occasions.

During Bill's tenure, the choir was accompanied by several pianists including Kathy Schnarr, Janet Duiker and Rosalyn Rosher. In 1988 Rosalyn took over as choir director with Beth Schiemann accompanying, followed by Janet Duiker.

The Senior Choir has continued to sing music of a more traditional and classical nature. In recent years, on occasion, they have combined with the Rejoice Choir to celebrate special services like the Sod Turning Ceremony and the dedication of the new sanctuary. They also sang for a Seminary Graduation Service held in our church and more recently for the televising of "Meeting Place" on Sunday, April 5, 1992.

Both choirs have also continued to support community events, singing at Rotary Carolfests, presenting the Christmas story to a visiting Japanese delegation and singing for the Opening and Closing Ceremonies of the Alberta Zone V Summer Games.

Senior Choir Director Rosalyn Rosher

Rejoice Choir

In 1978, 1 was approached by the Director of Christian Education, Ken Olson, to assist in forming a youth singing group. This group was formed to involve the young people in the church services, to praise the Lord.

After this group was formed, Ken Olson saw the need for an appropriate name for this new group. All of the youth were asked to choose a name. Each member presented an idea and wrote "his/her suggestion" on a large sheet of paper. Out of these many suggestions, Michelle Schoepp's "Rejoice" was chosen.

One of the most memorable times with the youth choir was the first concert on April 27, 1980. The members were asked to choose their favorite selections and explain to the audience what they meant to them. There was much sharing of personal faith and feeling.

Our second concert was held on May 29, 1983. The selection was "Come Trust the Lord" medley.

In 1985, the faces of the choir changed, as many of the youth graduated. The "Rejoice Choir" became a choir for all ages.

In 1986, we travelled to Emmaus, Drayton Valley to join their choir on their 30th Anniversary. Almost every May 24th long weekend was an opportunity to join the camp at Lake Isle in their "kick-off" service.

I am thankful for the opportunity to have served the Lord as director for 12 years and pray for continued blessings on the choir under the direction of Rev. Bill Ney.

Choir Director
Mary Schuman

Thoughts on the Rejoice Choir by Rev. Bill Ney

I took over as director of the Rejoice Choir in 1991 and have now led the choir for three years. Those three years are full of many fond and happy memories of times the Rejoice Choir sang at St. Matthew and also at other churches. For instance, I recall our singing for Bethlehem Lutheran Church in Edmonton, in the spring of '91 and the great reception we received from the members. A warm letter of thanks was also received from their pastor, Rev. Dorn, who indicated the gratefulness of his members for the quality music we provided. Riding in together on Ed Glubish's bus and then back home again after stopping for lunch at an Edmonton restaurant, was a part of the fun of that outing.

The devotions and prayers that we have shared together weekly as a choir have been a read source of strength for us as we focused on the blessings of God to us and requested that He might make us a blessing to others whenever we would sing.

The Rejoice Choir has been and continues to be really more than just a group of people who get together to sing. A closeness that is characterized by loving concern for each other has developed over the years and quickly encompasses anyone who becomes a part of the choir. This close relationship is fostered by special gatherings that are always memorable. The annual Christmas Party and the Spring Picnic are times of fun and fellowship always enjoyed by all.

The Rejoice Choir sees the 100th Anniversary of St. Matthew as a time to give thanks to God for His innumerable blessings in the past and a time to eagerly anticipate God's blessings in the future. We are happy to be able to be a part of a renewed ministry for the 21st century as we sing about God's work of redemption of mankind accomplished by the life, death and resurrection of Jesus Christ our Saviour so long ago. It is the hope that comes from His saving grace that we, as a choir, will continue to proclaim today, and on into the future, as long as God wills.

Rev. William R.A. Ney, Director,
St. Matthew Rejoice Choir

Vicars and Seminary Students

John "Jack" Stoop

Jack was born the oldest of three children in New York City, U.S.A, and is from a Dutch-German heritage. He was raised by parents who believe that a strong faith in God was most important. After graduating from Martin Luther High School in 1966, he attended Concordia College, Bronxville, where he met his wife Carol. They were married in August, 1969.

Jack and Carol spent time in California, Nebraska (where he attended Concordia Teachers' College, Seward), and Iowa. Jack served as Director of Christian Education, teacher, public school principal, and in the fields of bank management and financial consulting. In 1990, Jack entered the colloquy program at Concordia Seminary in Edmonton.

Jack served as a vicar at St. Matthew from May to August 1991. Jack, Carol and their two sons, Michael and Brian were also members of St. Matthew congregation.

Jack, Carol and their family presently live near Wetaskiwin where Jack is serving the congregations of Usona and Emmaus, Wetaskiwin.

Bruce Corson

Bruce was born April 6, 1955, in Quincy, California. He grew up in the surrounding area until moving to Idaho in 1979. Having completed his university schooling, and took a position for Clear Springs Trout Company raising Rainbow Trout. In 1982, he married Mary Clark and 2 years later they had their first child, Carrie. Bruce gradually worked his way through the ranks to a management position for the company and 2 more children were gifted to them, Leah and Philip. It was shortly after Philip's birth that Bruce felt a strong sense, through the small prayer group they were active in, to search for a way to serve the Lord. The doors were opened to attend Concordia Lutheran Seminary in August of 1990. After moving to the Adam's farm (John and Ruth) to live in Brenda Rockney's mobile home, Bruce was assigned as a field worker to St. Matthew Lutheran Church. This assignment was for 2 years, after which a move took place to Melfort, Saskatchewan for his vicarage placement. They hope to return to the Stony Plain area in 1993 to complete the last year of Seminary.

Seminary Field Workers

Brian Rosnau

Brian, Bev, Scott and Natasha Rosnau were members of St. Matthew Lutheran Church. Bev taught at St. Matthew School until Brian's graduation from the seminary in 1991. Brian is presently the pastor at Fort Qu'Appelle, Saskatchewan.

Gordon Heselton

Gordon, Naomi, Gabrielle, Daniel, Jonathan and Joshua Heselton were involved in the activities of the church and school which their children attended. Upon graduating in 1992, they moved to Mellowdale, Alberta where Gordon is presently serving as pastor.

Bruce Corson

Bruce, from Quincy, California, relocated to Idaho where he met and married Mary. They were blessed with three children - Carrie, Leah and Philip. In search of a way to further serve the Lord, they decided to move to the Stony Plain area so that Bruce could attend the seminary. He is now serving his first parish, St. Paul's Lutheran Church, Dawson Creek, B.C.

Benno Dreger

Benno frequently helped out in the choir and was involved in the youth ministry at St. Matthew Church. He married Carol Lehmann in 1992 just prior to his vicarage at Redeemer Lutheran Church in Edmonton. His first call was to be assistant pastor at St. Matthew Lutheran Church, Calgary.

Ken Edel

Ken was our field worker from September, 1993 to June, 1994. He took part in the worship services helping with the liturgy and preaching a few times. He attended youth meetings and assisted with some of their activities. He was assigned as vicar to Bethel Lutheran Church, Vulcan and Good Shepherd Lutheran Church, Calgary.

Jonathan Kraemer

Jonathan, our present field worker, is involved in many aspects of ministry, including Bible Studies, youth group, youth choir, assisting with the liturgy, and occasional preaching.

In Conclusion ...

We praise God for each and every one of these men and their families. All served in various capacities at St. Matthew and we are richer for their service. May God bless them in their future endeavors.

Schools

Images or Early and Present-day Schools

School No. 1 built in 1913

School No. 2 built in 1924

The present-day school built in 1954

Plans Made for Building of New School

June 25, 1950
At a special congregational meeting, it was decided to move school #1 to the Town of Stony Plain and amalgamate this with school #2 to be divided into junior and senior grades.

April 30, 1952
Educational survey and planning committee elected to investigate educational system of congregation.

January 20, 1954
At annual meeting a resolution was made and passed to begin construction on new school in spring. Cost estimate was put at $55,000, plus free labor. A loan of $25,000 be negotiated with "The District Church Extension Fund" or "The Bank of Commerce". By this time members of the congregation had pledged the total sum of $20,160.

July 5, 1954
80 men turn out to pour concrete for the foundation, all in one day.

November 14, 1954
The new school was dedicated on this day. Dr. H.J. Boettcher of Chicago, former teacher of St. Matthew, served as guest speaker in the afternoon dedication service.

November 29, 1954
First day of school in the new structure was a day of rejoicing for the school children and the teachers.

1959-1960
The school term began with a total enrolment of 114 pupils.

1960-1961
The school term began with a total enrolment of 119 pupils.

1967-1968
Enrolment at school, 121 pupils.

1976-1977
Enrolment at school, 128 pupils, of whom 60 were non-members.

1980-1981
Enrolment at school, 185 pupils.

1992-1993
Kindergarten to grade nine, 168 pupils, plus 36 children in playschool.

The start of school No 3 with the digging of the basement in 1954. Mr. Peter Janzen, contractor, is seen holding the elevation pole.

After the digging was completed, building the forms for the foundation was the next step.

Eighty men at work pouring concrete into the constructed forms at the school site in 1954.

Workmen at the school construction pouring more and more concrete.

Long-time members of St. Matthew (L-R) Gus Seehagel and Jacob Hennig helping in the building process.

St. Matthew Lutheran School

1984 - Present

Our School has seen many changes within its walls. Three labs have been added to meet the needs of the junior high department. These included a partially equipped Science Lab, a Computer Lab and a Home-Ec Lab.

The basement was renovated to accommodate grade nine. Two Sunday School rooms were made into one large classroom. The old libraiy/kindergarten room was separated by a wall to house Grade 8 and 9.

The outside of the building has been renovated to enhance the outside appearance and reduce over-heating in the summer months.

Playground equipment, asphalt and picnic tables were purchased by PTL for the enjoyment of the student body. Donations provided our staff room with a comfortable atmosphere for meetings, devotions and guests. Our librarian, Gloria Evjen, and her husband Merv, were the major force behind renovating our library.

We celebrated seventy-five years of Christian education in 1986. Our float won 1st place in the Farmer's Day Parade. Dignitaries and past teachers were among the invited guests at our Celebration Tea. Lutheran Life presented the school with a cheque to be used to purchase ten Apple computers.

Grade nine was implemented in 1985.

St. Matthew Lutheran School Principals

Daryl Becker:
-Concordia, Edmonton Graduate.
-Concordia, Seward, Nebraska - BSc.
- Presently working on Masters at River Forest, Chicago and is principal for Prince of Peace in Calgary, Alberta.

Daryl and his wife Lynne, of 15 years, are proud parents of Leah 10, Christopher 9, Cory 6 and Stacey 1.

Daryl was instrumental in implementing Grade Nine and daily remedial classes. Both programs are still offered at St. Matthew Lutheran School.

Alvin Clark:
Alvin graduated from the University of Calgary. He taught in southern Alberta for 15 years. He was a construction contractor before accepting the position at St. Matthew.

He has been married to Betty for more than thirty years. He has two children and resides in Sherwood Park.

Alvin initiated the computer lab after Lutheran Life donated the funds in honor of our 75th Anniversary. He was also instrumental in separating the Junior High into three distinct grades.

Wendy Fraser:
Wendy graduated from Seward, Nebraska and began teaching in a Lutheran school in the United States. Upon receiving a joint call, she and Bill moved to Stony Plain. Wendy taught Kindergarten and "retired" to raise her family.

In 1986, Wendy was called to teach again at St. Matthew. In 1989, she was appointed principal. Wendy has been married to Bill for 24 years. They are proud parents of three children: Lara, an Education student at Concordia College; Wil and David attending Concordia High School. Wendy became a Canadian citizen in April, 1990.

Wendy has increased and enriched the number of the Complimentary Courses offered to the Junior High at St. Matthew. She has encouraged expansion of classrooms to accommodate the class sizes.

Respectfully submitted, Wendy Fraser,

Principal.

Teachers
1984 - 1994

Anita Easton: 1983 - 1987 Coppermine, NWT.

Kathy Patrick: 1984 -1985 Calahoo, Alberta.

Sue Yelden: 1978 - 1988 Teacher - Fowler, Michigan

Linda Nikolaj: 1983 - 1986 Teacher - Concordia, Edmonton

Marilyn Quast: 1979 -1988 Admissions Concordia, Edmonton

Brenda Rockney: 1983 -1989 deceased June 27, 1991

Daryl Becker: 1982 - 1987 Principal - Calgary, Alberta

Debbie Stresman: 1986 - 1990 St. Catharine's, Ontario

Marilyn Witte: January, 1987 - 1991 All Saints, Edmonton

Todd Wandio: January, 1987 - June, 1991. Then teacher at Blueberry School near Stony Plain, Alberta

Alvin Clark: 1986 - 1988 Sherwood Park, Alberta

Ed Schnellert: 1987 - 1990 Teacher of Music - Kelowna, BC

Beverley Rosnau: 1987 - 1991 Fort Qu'Apelle, Sask.

Corinne Nowoczin: 1991 - March 1993 Secretary- Concordia Seminary, Edmonton, Alberta

Beth Schiemann: 1992 - 1993 (interim months)

Carolynne Herfindahl: 1988 - 1993, Edmonton.

Anika Ladoski: 1991-1994 Stony Plain, Alberta

Rosalyn Rosher: 1985-1994, Principal, Kelowna, B.C.

Present Staff:

Debbie Robin: 1990 - present Playschool

Jonathan Stanfel: 1989 - present Jr. High Science

Arlyn Belden: 1990 - present Grade 1/2 Beverley Adam: 1991 - present Jr. High Language Arts

Eric Ladoski: 1989 - present Grade 4

Elly van den Brande: 1980 - present Grade 5/6

Wendy Fraser: 1986 - present Principal/Grade 2/Jr. High.

Wendy Robinson: 1994 - Kindergarten and Grade 3

Cliff Opheim: 1994 -Grade 3.

Principals:

Daryl Becker 1983 - 1986

Alvin Clark 1986 - 1988

Wendy Fraser 1988 - Present

Support Staff:

Gloria Giese: Secretary 1984-1988

Sherley Gabel: Secretary 1988-1994

Connie Adam: Secretary 1994-Present

Dave Easton: Custodian 1983-1987

Doug Quinn: Custodian 1987-Present

St. Matthew School Teaching Staff for 1992-93

St. Matthew Lutheran School Teaching Staff of 1987-88

St. Matthew Lutheran School Parent Teacher League (PTL) 1984-1994

The Parent Teacher League of St. Matthew Lutheran School was formed to keep parents informed about the everyday business of running the school. It also serves as a communication link between staff and parents.

The group meets the second Tuesday of the month. Guest speakers present a wide range of informative topics, followed by the business portion of the meeting.

As well as holding monthly meetings, the PTL offers many other activities. It plans social get-togethers and, through various fundraisers, provides money for items needed at the school. It is also responsible for compiling the School Handbook, arranging for speakers for the meetings and overseeing the school's Hot Dog Days.

Over the past ten years, we have had a number of dedicated presidents. These volunteers were Mrs. Wanda Bourne, Mr. Bill Fraser, Mrs. Sherley Gabel, Mrs. Debbie Goertz, Mrs. Joyce Troudt, Mr. Wayne Whiteside and Mrs. Diane Lutz.

PTL has hosted different types of social events. We have had car rallies, baseball games, golf tournaments and Christmas craft evenings. We have also witnessed to the community through our floats in the Farmer's Day Parade.

Fundraising is one of PTL's more time consuming jobs. Fundraisers such as pie booths, spell-athons and sales of various candies and wrapping paper have proved successful. Proceeds from these sales have resulted in the purchase of items such as carpeting for the classrooms, a sound system, picnic tables, playground equipment, basketball nets, and most recently, two IBM compatible computers for our computer lab.

The cooperation of staff and parents has been a blessing to our school.

National Lutheran Parent-Teacher League

THIS CHARTER is presented to:

[signature]

[handwritten text]

who are members of the NATIONAL LUTHERAN PARENT-TEACHER LEAGUE and will carry out its purpose of helping parents and teachers to achieve greater competence in Christian child training and foster closer home-school-church relations.

[signature]
_____
Date

NATIONAL LUTHERAN PARENT-TEACHER LEAGUE

[signature]
_____
President

"Bring them up in the Nurture and Admonition of the Lord." Ephesians 6:4

98

Church

This small structure is the
replica of the 1899 church
shown below.

This is the 1899 St. Matthew Lutheran Church building located south-east of Stony Plain

The Building Committee Report

Hello to our brothers and sisters in Christ from your Building Committee.

The year 1989 has been very busy for all of us. We broke ground for our expansion on April 2. Construction went slowly from the offset. However, this was most likely the Lord's way of letting us keep up with everything. Work on the project is now moving quite rapidly as we can see progress almost daily. All of us on the building committee are looking forward to the completion of the project.

Labour assistance from the congregation has been significant. Through 1989, congregational help has been in excess of 2,000 man hours for which less than half has been charged. Also there has been about $13,000 worth of machine time used from congregational members. Much of this cost was not billed to the project. The financial support of the congregation has been terrific and is reported elsewhere in the annual report.

We also are most thankful for the greatest support of all, your prayers to the Lord for help and His answering those prayers by supporting us each moment of every day. ThankYou!

In 1990 we look to completing the construction phase of our expansion. We ask you to continue with your physical, financial and prayerful support. As we move from the construction phase of expansion into the outreach to people and souls, your active support and prayers will be even more important. Thank you again for your support.

In Christ's service for the Building Committee,

by Ivan G. Boles (As found in the 1989 congregational yearbook)

(L-R) John Adam, Glenn Stresmann, John Armbruster, Roland Hennig, Andy Gjevre, Ivan Boles, Stan Shwed, Murray Framingham, Richard Mohr and Garry Kulak are the members of the Building Committee for the new sanctuary.

Building the Temple

The Augsburg Confession defines the church as "the assembly of believers among whom the Gospel is preached in its purity and the holy sacraments are administered according to the Gospel." (AC, VII, 1) Dr. C.F.W. Walther says, "The church in the proper sense of the term is the congregation of saints, that is, the aggregate of all those who, called out of the lost and condemned human race by the Holy Spirit through the Word, truly believe in Christ and by faith are sanctified and incorporated in Christ." (Church and Ministry, CPH 1987, p. 19) This community of believers is built upon Jesus Christ and His Word as our Lord says, " ....on this rock I will build my church." (St. Matthew 16:18)

Rev. Carl Beiderwieden, the guest preacher at the Anniversary Service, spoke about building the church, the assembly of believers. He said that the "Word of the Great Salvation," the Gospel of Jesus Christ, builds the church. Pastor Beiderwieden said,

"And this is the way that the visible church has been built - this is its history - passing that Word of the Great Salvation from parents to children, from generation to

generation, from century to century. As each soul is made to lay hold on that Word another stone is added to the structure of the church. This is the only way that the church has been built, the only way that it can ever be built. We can

have church-growth programs, and evangelism outreaches, and stewardship seminars - and they are all good in themselves - but if they do not have as their one objective the passing of the Word about the Great Salvation then they are useless. Only that Word builds the church."

(A copy of his sermon is printed elsewhere in this book.) The Church is the community of saints gathered around the Word and the Sacraments.

This Church, the saints, build structures we call "churches." Why are these church buildings built? They are built in order to serve the proclamation of the Gospel and the administration of both Sacraments: the Sacrament of Baptism, and the Sacrament of the Altar. As the word of God is read and proclaimed in the church building to the community of saints, the church is built up and strengthened in their faith. When a child is baptized at the church building on Sunday morning, the infant becomes a member of the true church. As the believers gather at the Lord's Table and receive His true body and blood, they receive forgiveness and the church is strengthened. As the Augsburg Confession points out, the church is "the assembly of the believers among whom the Gospel is preached in its purity and the holy sacraments are administered according to the Gospel." Therefore, in order that the Word might be proclaimed and the Sacraments administered, the people of God (the church) build churches.

Another reason for building a church is outreach. The people of God have a mission to accomplish. They are to reach out to the unbelievers with the "Word of the Great Salvation." Again, the physical church structure is a tool used by the church to "make disciples of all nations." (St. Matthew 28:19) It is the Word of God that calls people out of the darkness of sin and into the light of the Gospel. St. Paul says that faith comes by hearing the Word of God. (Romans 10: 17) Within the walls of the church, this word of God is read and taught to the believers so that they are empowered to leave the building and share the Gospel with their neighbours, relatives, co-workers, and friends.

There are many other reasons for building a church, but only one more will be covered in this article. The church builds a church in order to glorify God. The Lord pours out his rich and abundant blessings upon His people and one of the ways of responding to His love is building a church that glorifies him for His goodness. St. Matthew Lutheran Church - the building - is a reflection of the love of its members for our Lord Jesus Christ. The building was not to be a testimony to man's accomplishments or to be a source of human pride. Instead, it was built as a testimony to God's great

accomplishment of salvation, and to be a source of praise and thanksgiving to God.

When the temple in Jerusalem was completed, King David prayed these words:

"But who am I, and who are my people, that we should be able to give as generously as this? Everything comes from you, and we have given you only what comes from your hand .... O Lord our God, as for all this abundance that we have provided for building you a temple for your Holy Name, it comes from your hand, and all of it belongs to you. "

(1 Chronicles 29: 14-16)

Roger M. Sedlmayr, Pastor
February 1, 1995

Church Building Program 1985-1990

April 21, 1985
Building planning committee formed by a motion at a congregational meeting.

November 17,1985
Building planning committee presents a report at a congregational meeting.

November 25, 1985
Resolution passed by congregation to plan and construct an addition to the existing building.

Spring, 1986
Building finance committee carries out an every-member visit program for financial commitments to the building program.

August 27, 1986
The committees presented their final reports to the congregational meeting.

March 8, 1987
Congregation adopts two resolutions:
1st. To do own contracting by hiring a project manager.
2nd. To begin construction when $500,000 was on hand. Gordon Lander was hired as project manager.

February 15,1989
Project manager begins his duties. By now $600,000 was raised and the decision made to proceed with the building project.

April 2, 1989
Ground breaking service was held.

April 6, 1989
The parsonage, built in 1947, was demolished and removed.

April 12, 1989
Excavation for addition starts.

May 13, 1990
Last service held in old church.

May 20, 1990
Cornerstone is dedicated on this day, and the first service held in the new addition.

June 17,1990
New house of worship is dedicated to the Glory of God. Rev. Murvyn Kentel, former pastor at St. Matthew Lutheran, served as guest speaker at the morning service. Dr. Edwin Lehman, President of Lutheran Church - Canada, was the speaker at the 2:30 p.m. service. Approximately 1500 people attended the two services.

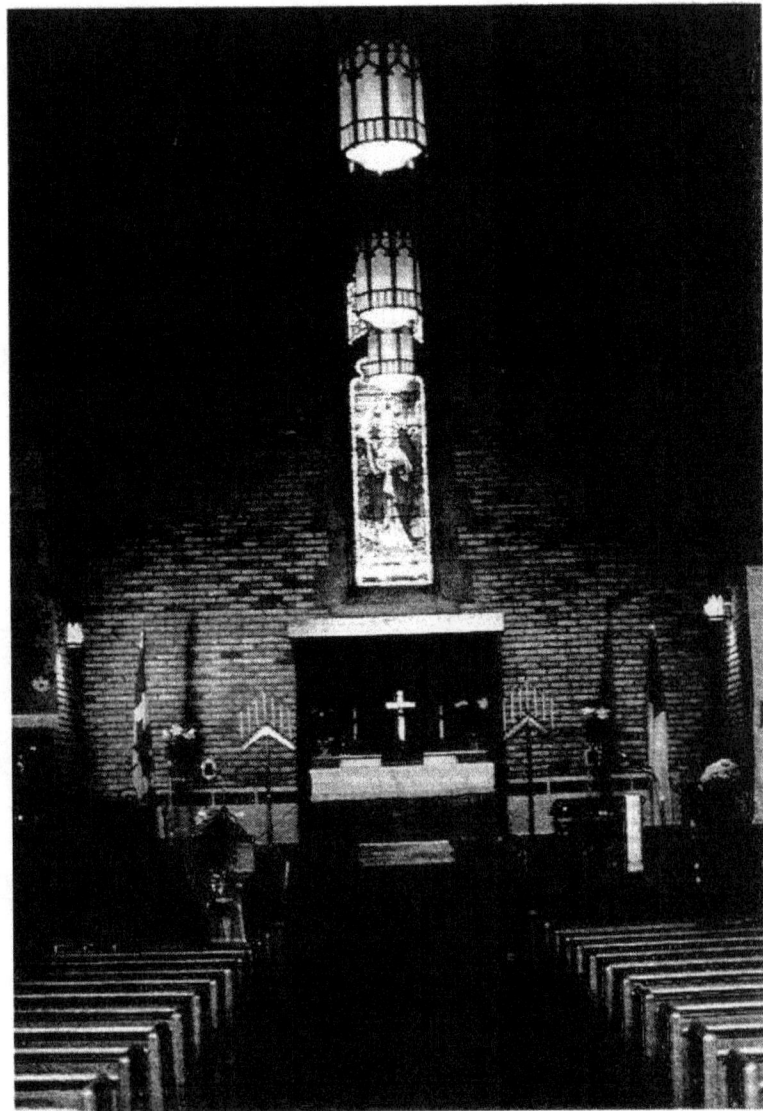

Interior view of the 1949 church sanctuary

The Pictorial Diary of the Church Building Program

The following pictures clearly capture the development and process of the construction of the new sanctuary.
Much preparation, planning and praying has gone into this work. Through this photographic record, it is clear to see the team work that was in evidence and so very necessary in order to bring this work to completion. We ore so very grateful for all the helping hands that shared and gave so willingly. We do have cause to praise and thank God for our people, the leadership, and our faithful servants who labour in the cause of a crucified and risen Lord.

Building Project Sign - March 30, 1989

Project Manager Gordon Lander hired October 17, 1989

Snow Removal for ground breaking - March 25, 1989

Thawing ground for ground breaking ceremony - March 31, 1989. Pictured are Pastor Shieman and Marvin Hennig

The ground breaking ceremony on April 2, 1989 with Pastors Don Schieman and Harold Witte

Demolition of Parsonage, April 6, 1989

The beginning of excavation - April 12, 1989

Preparation for footings - May 19, 1989

Pouring concrete for the basement walls - June 1, 1989

...moving stone ve... ...el - facing west on July 7, 1989

Preliminary stage of
construction -
September 13, 1989

Upper view of rafters October 2, 1989

---->

Placing rafters by crane-
October 5, 1989   ----->

Exterior view of main entrance in progress - October 17, 1989

Entrance to worship area under construction - November 23, 1989

113

Placing marble and tile in Sanctuary- Bill Getzinger February 9, 1990

Attaching trim from scafolding in Narthex March 12, 1990

South windows in Narthex, January 12, 1990

Installing doors to worship area, February 9, 1990

Distant view of Altar area

Workmen plastering south view of new addition - April 3, 1990

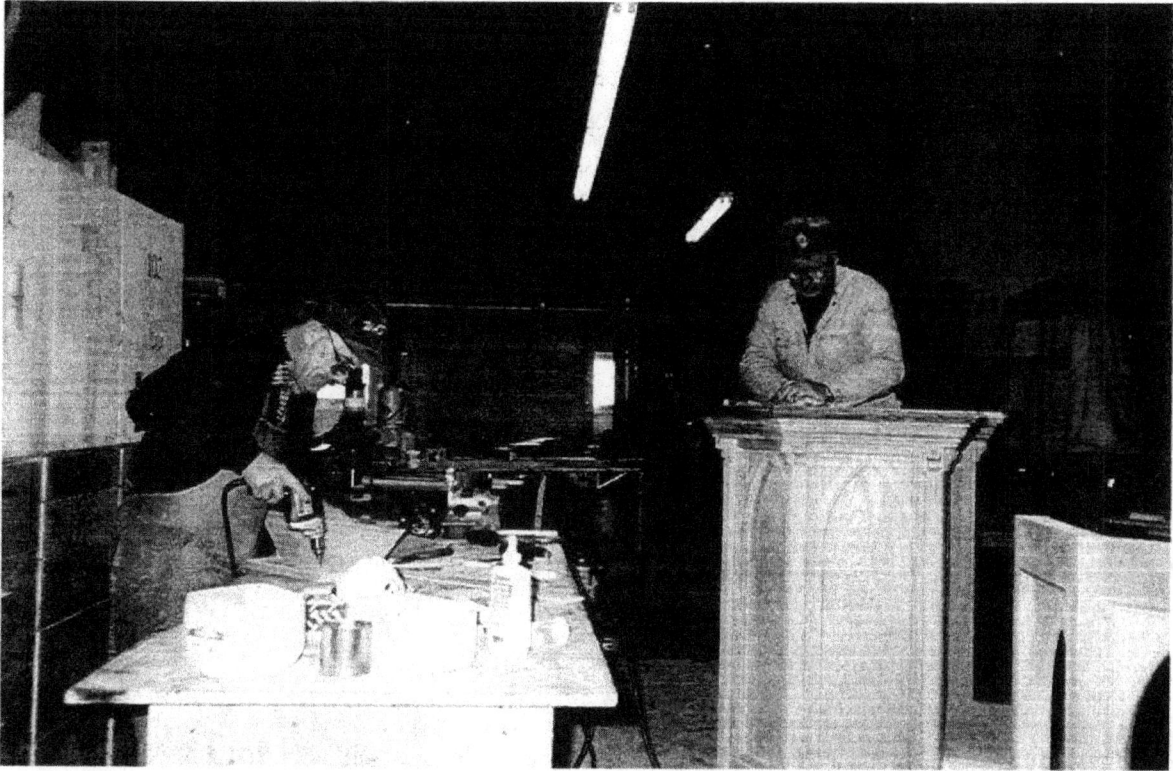

Altar furnishings under construction: Wally Steinbring   (left) - March 6, 1990

Construction of Communion   Table under way - March 6, 1990

Altar furnishings ready for placement - May 11, 1990

Workers assembling new pews - May 11, 1990

Workers placing pews - May 11, 1990

Congregational procession to the new Sanctuary for first service - May 20, 1990

Cornerstone laying - (L-R) Ivan Boles and Gordon Lander - May 20, 1990

First service in new Sanctuary - May 20, 1990

First Baptism (Double) Leah Unterschultz (Parents Allan and Elaine) and Braeden Mayer (Parents Perry and Terry) - May 20, 1990

Pastor Schlemann conducting object lesson for the children - May 20, 1990

**Pastor Schiemann officiating at first wedding
for Nadine Ulmer and Marcel Melanson - June 16, 1990**

Combination of Old Church (October 31, 1949) and New Addition (June 17, 1990)

Following is a record of all donations made to this time:

DONATIONS OF VARIOUS FURNISHINGS

ALTAR: with sincere thanks for a lifetime of love, kindness, understanding, and leading their family in worship of our Triune Lord; as well as showing us the Grace of Jesus Christ; the Altar is donated in loving gratitude and thanks by the family of, in the name of Walter (Tecky) and Mary Doern.

PULPIT: by Roland- and Bernice Hennig and family in loving memory of Jacob and Elizabeth Hennig.

LECTERN: by Mrs. Hilda Gehring and family in loving memory of Rev. Arthur Gehring.

BAPTISMAL FONT: by Mrs. Elsie J. Smith, Bryan and Bev Adam in loving memory of Harold Smith.

1 PEW: by Mrs. Theresia Goebel and family in loving memory of Emil J. Goebel.

1 PEW: by Mrs. Elsie M. Kulak and family in loving memory of Valentine and Elizabeth Hennig.

1 CHOIR CHAIR: by Mrs. Elsie M. Kulak and family in loving memory of Henry J. Kulak.-

1 PEW: by Mrs. Emilie (Pat) Enders in loving memory of Philip J. - -Enders. --- — ...

1 PEW: by Miss Julia Ulmer in loving memory of Mrs. Lydia Woodley.

1 PEW; by Mrs. Erna Lutz and family in loving memory of Arthur Lutz.

2 .PEWS: by John and Ruth Adam in loving memory of Mrs. Katherine Goertz.

Mary Hemmelgarn.

2 PEWS: by the Fielhaber family in loving memory of George and Elizabeth Fielhaber. -------------------- --- --- ---- — . _ . ...

ALTAR LINEN & PARAMENTS; by the Altar Guild of St. Matthew.

1 PEW; by Miss Emelia P. Hennig in loving memory of Valentine and Elizabeth Hennig.

1 CHOIR CHAIR: by Mrs. Clara Evjen in loving memory of John Evjen.

2 CHOIR CHAIRS; by Mrs. Louise Raduenz, Sr. in loving memory of Rev. Alvin H. Raduenz.

1 CHOIR CHAIR: by Miss Beverly Hennig in loving memory of Jacob and Elizabeth Hennig.

1 PEW; by Carl and Ruth Schutz in loving memory of Philip & Christine Schutz and Louis & Elizabeth Kulak.

1 PEW; by Albert and Rita Seehagel and family in loving memory of Gus and Barbara Seehagel.

HYMN BOARDS: by Jim and Hilda Quinn in loving memory of Marianne Varaleau.

1 PEW; by Louis and Katherine Steuber in loving memory of Louis and Maria Steuber, and Adam and Caroline Getzinger.

1 PEW: by the Doern family in loving memory of Jacob and Maria J. Doern.

1 CHOIR CHAIR: by John and Ruth Adam in loving memory of Jacob and Elizabeth Hennig.

SHARED PEW: by Gus and Lydia Getzinger in loving memory of Adam & Caroline Getzinger and Andrew & Margaret Schultz.

SHARED PEW: by Cecil Woodley in loving memory of Lydia Woodley.

1 CHOIR CHAIR: by Marvin and Rose Hennig and family in loving memory of Katherine Goertz.

1 PEW: by Albert and Waltraut Wendel and family in loving memory of Joseph Kulak.

1 PEW: by Philip and Victor Getzinger in loving memory of Emma Getzinger.

1 PEW: by Jack and Martha Dringenberg in loving memory of Ed and Magdalina Dringenberg, and William and Elizabeth Graf.

1 CHOIR CHAIR: by Mrs. Ida Pearce in loving memory of Rev. E. Geo. Pearce.

2 CHOIR CHAIRS; by Mrs. Rose Enders in loving memory of Philip L. Enders.

1 PEW: by Henry, Meta and Eric Getzinger in loving memory of Miss Linda Getzinger.

2 CHOIR CHAIRS: by Alfred and Doreen Altheim in loving memory of John and Katherine Schutz and sister Lorrinda.

1 CHOIR CHAIR: by Mrs. Miriam Robson in loving memory of Leslie E. Robson.

1 CHOIR CHAIR: by Mrs. Rosalyn Rosher in loving memory of Leslie E. Robson.

1 PEW: by Mrs. Mary Schutz in loving memory of Philip C. Schutz.

1 PEW: by Carl & Norma Baron, Mrs. Emma Ulmer, Barney & Tillie Springman in loving memory of Carl and Elizabeth Baron.

1 PEW: by Emil and Frieda Miller and family in loving memory of Valentine & Caroline Miller, and David Shepherd.

1 PEW: by Mrs. Emma Ulmer and family in loving memory of Leonard Ulmer.

1 CHOIR CHAIR: by Eric and Connie Pedersen in loving memory of Jacob and Mary Altheim.

SHARED PEW: by Mrs. Viola Irwin in loving memory of George and Louise Rehkopf.

SHARED PEW: by Mrs. Elizabeth Schienbein in loving memory of Carl Schienbein, and Andrew and Margaret Schultz.

1 PEW: by Mrs. Katherine Schutz and family in loving memory of Henry P. Schutz.

1 CHOIR CHAIR: by Pastor Don and Mrs. Beth Schiemann and family in loving memory of Miss Kathy Israel.

1 CHOIR CHAIR: by Pastor Don and Mrs. Beth Schiemann and family in loving memory of Rev. Fred and Mrs. Emma Schiemann.

SHARED PEW; by Walter, Sr. and Frieda Schulze.

SHARED PEW: by Mrs. Theresia Schram in loving memory of Christian & Caroline Hennig.

1 PEW: by Mrs. Mary Brown in loving memory of Harold G. Brown, and Henry & Theresia Enders.

1 PEW: by Walter and Mary Doern and family in loving memory of Jacob and Elizabeth Hennig.

1 PEW; by Miss Hedwig Schienbein in loving memory of Adam and Barbara Schienbein.

2 CHOIR CHAIRS: by Sidney and Judy Kulak in loving memory of Henry and Emma Kulak.

1 CHOIR CHAIR: by Mrs. Marie Propp in loving memory of Carl Propp.

1 CHOIR CHAIR: by Robert and Cleone Goldsack in loving memory of Carl Propp.

J. PEW: by Harvey and Laurraine Hennig and family in loving memory of Emil and Martha Hennig.

5 CHOIR CHAIRS, LC-C and CANADIAN FLAGS: "To the Glory of God and Thanksgiving for Blessings Received", by St. Matthew Youth.

1 PEW: by William and Herta Seehagel and family in loving memory of Gustav and Barbara Seehagel.

1 PEW: by Mrs. Emma Ulmer and family in loving memory of Carl & Elizabeth Baron, and Jacob Margaret Ulmer.

1 CHOIR CHAIR: by Mrs. Theresia Goebel in loving memory of Jacob and Maria Schoepp.

X PEW: by Miss Hedwig Schienbein in loving memory of Eleanor Kuhl.

<u>1</u> CHOIR CHAIR; by Jack and Dorothy Kulak in loving memory of Philip and
    Phillipina Kulak.
<u>2</u> <u>PEW</u>: by Herb P. and Esther Hennig "Dedicated to the Glory of God,
    who, thru His sacrificial love, has granted us and our family a
    steadfast faith, hope, protection, healing and many other daily
    blessings."
<u>1</u> <u>PEW</u>: by Mrs. Barbara Dreitza in loving memory of Fred Dreitza.
<u>X</u> <u>CHOIR CHAIR</u>: by Garry and Phyllis Kulak and family in loving memory of John
    Litzenberger.* .. . .
<u>SHARED PEW</u>: by Garry and Phyllis Kulak and family in loving memory of John
    Litzenberger.
<u>SHARED PEW</u>: by Edwin and Adele Ulmer in loving memory of Emil and Emily Modro
    (McLellan).
<u>X</u> <u>CHOIR CHAIR</u>: by Harold and Agnes Evjen in loving memory of Peter and
    Mathilda Evjen. .   ..
<u>X</u> <u>CHOIR CHAIR</u>: by Harold and Agnes Evjen in loving memory of Otto — - Evjen.
<u>1</u> <u>CHOI R CH AIR</u>: by Norman and Lucy Holt and family* in loving memory of
    Adele Holt.'. •.
<u>2</u> <u>CHOIR CHAIRS</u>: by Ted and Mary Schuman in loving memory of John and ;
    Johanna Metzger.'
<u>X</u> <u>CHOIR CHAIR</u>: by Belinda Framingham in loving memory-of Fred----------
    Framingham. •
<u>1</u> <u>PEW</u>: by Mrs. Martha Schoepp and family in loving memory of Jacob
    J. Schoepp.
<u>2</u> <u>CHOIR CHAIRS</u>: by Jeanette and Eric Steuber and family in loving memory of
    William Steuber.
<u>1</u> <u>CHOIR CHAIR</u>: by Ernie and Hilda Breitkreutz and family: "because of
• _ ___ His goodness_and everlasting mercy, we give thanks and praise
    to bur Triune God for hearing and .answering the. prayers of all,
    who in faith and trust, prayed for Ernie's continuing recovery".
<u>2</u> <u>PEW</u>: by Mrs. Emma Schellenberger and family in loving memory of
    Henry H. Schellenberger.
<u>3</u> <u>CHOIR CHAIRS</u>: by George Kuhl and family in loving memory of Eleanor Kuhl.
<u>1</u> <u>CHOIR CHAIR</u>: by Walter and Maxine Bauer.
<u>1</u> <u>PEW</u>: by Mrs. Aurelia Hennig and family in loving memory of Philip
    H. Hennig.
<u>2</u> <u>CHOIR CHAIRS</u>: by Walter M. and Anne Goertz.   '
<u>2</u> <u>CHOIR CHAIRS</u>: by Greg and Cheryl Wurz.-
<u>1</u> <u>CHOIR CHAIR</u>: by Bill and Linda Riedlinger in loving memory of Evelyn
    Reidlinger.
<u>3</u> <u>CHOIR CHAIRS</u>:' by Rheinold and Bertha Miskey in loving memory of Otto,
    Edward, Walter, and Oscar Miskey.
<u>4</u> <u>CHOIR CHAIRS</u>: by Mrs. Emma Goebel in loving memory of Louis J. Goebel.
<u>1</u> <u>PEW</u>: by Darrel and Jack Hennig, Roger and Heather Goerz in loving
    memory of Ted Wudel.
<u>CORNERSTONE PLAQUE</u>: by Otto C. Hennig in loving memory of Jacob and Elizabeth
    Hennig.
<u>CORNERSTONE BOX</u>: by Roland and Bernice Hennig in loving memory of Edward
    Hennig.
<u>ALTAR RAILING (1/2)</u>: by Otto C. Hennig and family in loving memory of Leona
    Hennig.
<u>ALTAR RAILING (1/2)</u>: by the Altheim family in loving memory of Jacob and Mary
    Altheim.
<u>SHARED PEW</u>: by Herman and Adele Steinke.
<u>1</u> <u>CHOIR CHAIR</u>: by Herman and Adele Steinke.
<u>1</u> <u>PEW</u>: by Stan and Gerri Schram and Wayne and Fran Schram and
    families in honor of Jack and Lydia Schram, "in appreciation
_ ... of the Lord's special acts of grace bestowed upon them through their
lifetime."
<u>1</u> CHOIR CHAIR; by Kim and Corliss Preece and family in loving memory of Leonard
    Ulmer.
<u>1</u> <u>CHOIR CHAIR</u>: by Ron and Debra Matiejewski and family in loving memory of
    Leonard Ulmer.

1 <u>CHOIR CHAIR</u>: by Randall and Susan Ulmer and family in loving memory of
Leonard Ulmer.

3 <u>CHOIR CHAIRS</u>: by Mrs. Minnie Schuttler in loving memory of Jacob and
Katherine Getzinger.

1 <u>PEW</u>:   by the Eberhardt family in loving memory of Dr. and Mrs. Emil
Eberhardt.

1 <u>PEW</u>:   by Mrs. Emma Litzenberger and family in loving memory of
Jacob P. Litzenberger.

<u>CEILING LITES</u> (set of four): by Allan and Diane Lutz and family in loving
memory of Arthur Lutz.

1 <u>PEW</u>:   by Mrs. Carrie Steinmetz in loving memory of Albert Steinmetz.

1 <u>PEW</u>:   by Henry Ducholke in loving memory of Mary Ducholke.

<u>SHARED PEW</u>: by Norman and Joyce Ducholke in honor of Henry and in loving memory
of Mary Ducholke.

<u>SHARED PEW</u>: by Ed and Evelyn Giese in honor of Henry and in loving
- memory of Mary Ducholke.   ....

<u>PRESENCE LITE</u>: by Glenn and Debra Stresman "In thanksgiving for God's blessings
to our family while we were members of St. Matthew"

<u>SHARED PEW</u>: by Mrs. Erna Giese in loving memory of Eric Giese and daughter
Grace.

<u>ETERNAL LITE</u>: by Pastor William and Diane Ney "in gratefulness to God for
countless blessings on - the occasion of their 20th Wedding
Anniversary Sept. 4, 1990".

1 <u>PEW</u>:   by the Kuhl family in loving memory of Edward and Emma Kuhl.

2 <u>PEW</u>:   by Werner and Florence Lemmer and family in loving memory of
Marie Lemmer (Damazyn).

<u>JL PEW</u>:   by Mrs. Elizabeth Goertz and family in loving memory of Oscar
....   Goertz-   --- --- ------- --

1 <u>PEW</u>:   by Eric'and Mildred Ulmer in loving memory of Louis J. and
Olga Ulmer & John and Maria Ulmer.:

2 <u>NARTHEX FANS</u>: by Emil and Tillie Altheim and family in loving memory of
Josie Bancroft.[1]

1 <u>PEW</u>:   by Richard and Eleanor Unterschultz and family in loving
memory of Jacob and Louise Unterschultz.

1.<u>PEW</u>:   by Irene Mayer and Eileen Gosset in honor of Emelia Wudel.

1 <u>PEW</u>:   by Richard and Judy Mohr & Henry and Tillie Mohr in loving
/ , •. memory of Henry and Elizabeth Goertz.

<u>X PEW</u>:   by Mrs. Katharine Mayer, Edward and Jack in loving memory of
Jacob Mayer Sr., and Fred Mayer.

<u>NARTHEX CARPET</u>: by Philip and Lydia Lutz in loving memory of Barbara Lane and
Carol Roy.

1 <u>PEW</u>:   by Mrs. Bertha Enders and family in loving memory of Henry L.
Enders.

2 <u>PEW</u>:   by Otto and Kay Goebel "in thankfulness to God for all His
blessings, mercy and love showered upon us and our families during
our lifetime."

<u>MISSAL STAND</u>: by Mrs. ClaraDucholke in loving memory of Edward F. Ducholke.

<u>CANDELABRA SHARED</u>: by Mrs. Edna Giese and family in loving memory of Edwin A.
Giese.

<u>CANDELABRA SHARED</u>; by Mrs. Salome Lutz and family in loving memory of Emil
Lutz.

<u>COMMUNION WARE</u>: by St. Matthew Ladies Aid in loving memory of, and to the
honor of Dr. Emil Eberhardt and his families.

<u>OFFERING PLATES AND WHEEL CHAIR RAMP RAIL</u> (Altar): by the members of the
Senior Bible Class in loving memory of the Senior members who have
gone to be with their Lord.

<u>COMMUNION RAIL KNEELERS</u>: by St. Matthew Ladies Aid in loving memory of
Margaret Goertz.   .....

<u>CHANCEL CROSS - DONATION</u>: by Bertha Ulmer in loving memory of Carl L. Ulmer
and sons Walter and infant.

<u>CHANCEL CROSS - DONATION</u>: by William and Evelyn Hohnstein in loving memory of

Carl L. Ulmer.

CHANCEL CROSS - DONATION: by Edwin and Adele Ulmer in loving memory of Carl
        L. Ulmer.

CHANCEL CROSS - DONATION: by the Ducholke family in loving memory of Edward
        F. Ducholke.

CLERGY CHAIRS: by the families of Walter Kupsch and Otto Burghardt "in
        thankfulness and praise to God for the many blessings showered on
        family and friends thru His servant Irene Kupsch {Burghardt} whose
        memory is ever cherished".

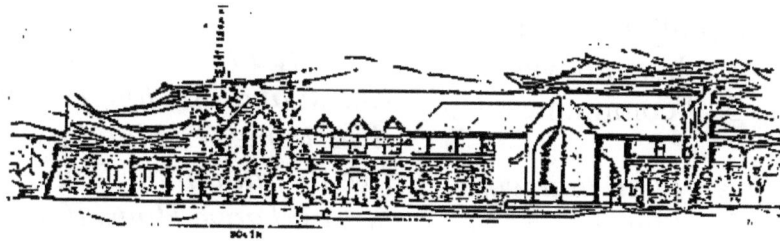

Fellow Servants of Jesus Christ

As we celebrate the 100th year of St. Matthew Evangelical Lutheran Church, there is much to be thankful for and much to look forward to.

In 1894, some 20 families founded St. Matthew Congregation. At that time the membership was 112 baptized, with 58 communicants.

In 1894, every member of the congregation was active both in weekly worship of the Lord, and in doing his or her share in serving the needs of the congregation. In this spirit of serving, the members of St. Matthew saw the congregation grow rapidly for the next 10 years. In 1904, membership was 645 baptized, including 349 communicants.

Romans 15:4 For everything that was written in the past (Scripture) was written to teach us; so that through endurance and the encouragement of the Scriptures we might have hope.

Proverbs 22:6 Train up a child in the way he should go and when he is old he will not turn from it.

Psalm 78:7 Then they would put their trust in God.

Christian education was, in 1894, is in 1994 and will be in the future, important to St. Matthew members. Scripture is the Lord's inspired message to us. If we, as children of God, accept the teachings of Scripture, we will all set our trust and hope in God for the future.

In 1994, the membership of St. Matthew stands at over 489 families, consisting of 1,104 baptized souls including 849 communicants. In the past 100 years, St. Matthew congregation has grown tenfold. This is good news indeed. However, we also must recognize that the community population has increased by a factor of over 100. We have a lot of work to do in extending the message of Jesus Christ.

3 Cor. 5:14-15 For Christ's love compels us, because we are convinced that one died for all, and therefore all died. And He died for all, that those who live should no longer live for themselves, but for Him who died for them, and was raised again.

Gal. 2:20 I have been crucified with Christ and I no longer live, but Christ lives in me. The life I live in the body, I live by faith in the Son of God, who loved me, and gave Himself for me.

How we live and serve Christ today and in the future is determined by our trust, hope and faith in Jesus Christ. Today, even though the membership at St. Matthew is large, there are not enough members willing to set aside enough time to do the work of the congregation. This situation moves us to consider the story of "Someone Else."

-The church was saddened this week to learn of the death of one of our most available members - SOMEONE ELSE.

-SOMEONE ELSE'S passing creates a vacancy which will be difficult to fill.

-SOMEONE ELSE did far more than

the normal person's share of the work.

Whenever there was a job to do, a class to teach, a meeting to attend, one name was on everyone's list: "Let SOMEONE ELSE do it."

-It was common knowledge that SOMEONE ELSE was among the largest givers in the church. Whenever there was a financial need, everyone just assumed that SOMEONE ELSE would make up the difference.

-SOMEONE ELSE was a wonderful person, sometimes appearing superhuman, but a person can only do so much. Were the truth known, everyone expected too much of SOMEONE ELSE.

-Now SOMEONE ELSE is gone! We wonder what we are going to do!

-SOMEONE ELSE left a wonderful example to follow, but who is going to do the things SOMEONE ELSE did?

-When you are asked to help, remember you can not depend on SOMEONE ELSE.

1 John 3:18 Dear children, let us not love with words or tongue, but with actions and in truth.

The SOMEONE ELSE part of this message is directed to each member of St. Matthew as individuals, rather than to the congregation as a whole. We, as individuals, must show our love of Christ not only in words but also in serving actions.

There is an urgency needed in these actions. When we, as individuals put off serving, it means SOMEONE ELSE must do what we have refused to do. In fact, what is happening, is that the church's work — the work of Christ's church — does not get done. We all have good excuses for refusing to work in Christ's Church. We are too busy with family, work, holidays, recreation, etc. However, remember that it is Christ who has given us familyjobs, holidays, recreation, etc. It is only reasonable that we should serve Christ's Church while we accept Christ's blessings.

As we consider how we can serve Christ in His Church, we will be part of a growing church for the next 100 years and more.

Praise God from whom all blessings flow.

In the service of Jesus Christ, Ivan G. Boles, Chairman

129

The Pictorial Review
of Historic Past
Up To 1994

St. Matthew Lutheran Church, Stony Plain, Alberta, 1994

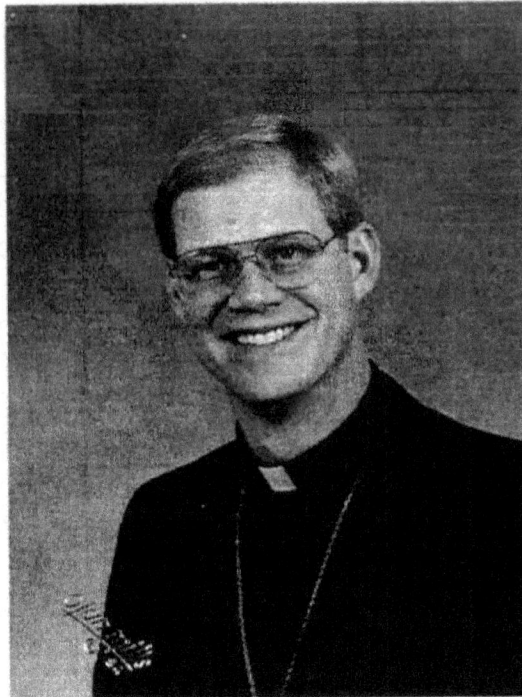

Rev. William Heine, Associate Pastor

Rev. Roger Sedlmayr, Senior Pastor

Preparing site for church sign * 1980
Pictured here are L-R Bill Hohnstein, Eric Baron and Roland Hennig

St. Matthew Lutheran Church Sign as of February 13, 1994

"The Lutheran Hour" sign on Highway #16 West near Stony Plain, Alberta

The last resting place for the missionary and founder of St. Matthew Lutheran Church
Rev. Dr. Emil E. Eberhardt buried in the St. Matthew Cemetery

Soccer Team for St. Matthew Lutheran   School #2 (circa 1938)

Rev. and Mrs. Eberhardt ready for a winter trip.

Rev. and Mrs. Eberhardt ready for a winter trip

St. Matthew slow pitch ball team - tournament at Golden, B.C. August 6-7, 1988

St. Matthew Church Band

St. Matthew Lutheran Church Band
Band Director Schumann (far left) withPastor Eberhardt wearing cap and fourth person L-R
This picture was taken about 1920

St. Matthew Church Band approximately 1922

The Confirmation Class of the early 1940's proceeding to the confirmation day service at the 1899 church next door. (Please Note: the Windcharger behind the parsonage which was used to generate electricity to supply lighting in both the church and parsonage.)

Gathering for Mission Fest at St. Matthew Church in the country about 1920's. (Please Note: the use of the Band shell occupied by the church serenading the onlookers and the Flag of the Union Jack symbolic of the loyalty of these people to king and country.)

The Senior Bible   Class of 1987

Pastors at the Rev. Harold Witte Installation, September 1984

The Young People's group on steps of St. Matthew School #2 in the early 1930's

Teacher Philip Enders' Class at St. Matthew School #2 in 1927

The St. Matthew Lutheran Church Parsonage in Stony Plain, 1984

The 50th Anniversary day of St. Matthew in 1944 outside of the 1899 church

'You are cordially invited to the

DEDICATION SERVICES

OF

St. Matthews Lutheran Church
Stony 'Plain, Alberta

ON

Sunday, the thirtieth of October, 1949

Morning Dedication (German)—10:30 o'clock
Afternoon Dedication (English)— 2:30 o'clock
Evening- Vespers (English)— 7:30 o'clock

This was the official invitation used for the dedication services of the 1949 Church

Carl Dubetz, the stone mason for the 1949 church, is seen here in the centre of the picture

along with his helpers

This is a rare photograph of the Eberhardt Family (L-R) George, Lydia, Pastor Eberhardt, and Anna in about 1925

St. Matthew Choir on the occasion of the 50th Anniversary in 1944, Walter Rosnau, director

St. Matthew School #2 pupils on hike along the railroad track in June,1934

Participants in a 1931 play presented by the Walther League players at St. Matthew

This is the interior long-view of the 1899 St. Matthew Lutheran Church

This was the congregational photograph for the 25th Anniversary of St. Matthew Congregation in 1919

Figure 3 In 1944 St. Matthew Lutheran congregation witnessed the celebration of its' 50th Anniversary.

Part Three

Confirmation
... something steadfast and sure

Pastor Emil Eberhardt with his Confirmation Class of 1928, the earliest available picture of confirmation

Rev. Roger Sedlmayr with his Confirmation Class of 1994 which
is the last confirmation class of the centennial

Pastor Emil E. Eberhardt with Confirmation Class of 1939

St. Matthew's last German language Confirmation Class of 1942. Pastor Eberhardt presiding.

Confirmation Class of 1947 with Pastor Philip Janz

St. Matthew Confirmation Class with Pastor Kentel and Pastor Witte in 1987

Confirmation Register

Confirm and 1985	Parent's Name
Shelley Anderson	Mrs. Pat A.
Cameron Goebel	Clifford G.
Kevin Kulak	Delmar K.
Tammy Menzies	Mrs. Geraldine Carruthers
Jeffrey Nilsson	Mrs. Carol N.
Vincent Osborne	Anthony O.
Darren Plunz	Ronald P.
Kevin Raduenz	Robert R.
Paula Schutz	Laurie S.
Warren Schutz	Rod S.
Mark Seehagel	William S.
Heidi Steiner	Ingnaz S.
Carl Topping	Roy T.
Audrey Velichka	Leonard V.
Nicholas Woodley	Wayne W.

Adult Class:
Russell Bardak
Chris Birrell
Kelly Doyle
Jim Quinn
Rosalyn Rosher
Linda Seeburger
Elaine Willoughby

1986	
Todd Ganske	Dwight G.
Shelley Getzinger	Rhiney G.
Kim Giese	Ronald G.
Glen Goebel	Jerry G.
Mark Hennig	Harvey H.
Diane Krushinsky	Cecil K.
Heidi Lemmer	Werner L.
Angela Nernberg	Kenneth N.
Russell Osborne	Anthony O.
Corinne Roberts	Roger R.
Charlene Schutz	Mrs. Jacoba S.
Leslie Steuber	Eric S.
Jody Topolnisky	Milton T.
Lisa Unterschultz	Richard U.
Tammy Unterschultz	Donald U.
Steven Whitlock	Don W.

Adult Class:
Cynthia Hohnstein
Victor Parfieniuk
Elaine Pipke
Richard Pipke

1987	
Lisa Baron	Robert B.
David Fritsen	Bill F.
Scott Fuhr	Wayne F.

Confirmand	Parent's Name
Vicky Getzinger	Victor G.
Cheryl Giese	Kenneth G.
Carmen Gjevre	Andrew G.
Brent Hennig	Harvey H.
David Kulak	Sidney K.
Kim Laramee	Roland L.
Jodi Luckhardt	Brian L.
Tamara Mohr	Richard M.
Joshua Quast	William Q.
Laura Rockney	Mrs. Brenda R.
Colin Schutz	Rod S.
Kane Schutz	Laurie S.
John Tomaino	Doran Bourne

Adult Class:
Jennifer Goebel
Debra Strei

1988	
Marsha Boychuk	Mrs. Donna B.
Trent Framingham	Murray F.
Chad Ganske	William F.
Dion Getzinger	Dwight G.
Tracy Giese	Rhiney G.
Doyle Miskey	Larry G.
Sheri Nernberg	Andrew M.
Jennifer Nilsson	Kenneth N.
Ted Polzin	Chris Birrell
Jeremy Quast	Thomas P.
Scott Rosnau	William Q.
Jason Schoepp	Brian R.
Sonja Steiner	Gerald S.
Harley	Ignaz S.
Danette Ursel	Milton T.
Jeffrey Whitlock	Gordon U.
Tammy Yacyshen	Don W.
	Mrs. Gladys Y.

Adult Class:
Shelly (Fisher)
Jean Hay Kevin
Hay Alfred
Kloeck
Sharon Kloeck
Wendy Knopke
Shelly Treit Bill
White
Greg Wurz

1989	
Kevin Achtzener	Norman A.
Michelle Altheim	David A.
Stephen Fritsen	Bill F.
Michael Giese	Kenneth G.
Michael Goebel	Gary G.
Donald Hennig	Harvey H.

Confirm and	Parent's	Confirmand	Parent's Name
Jason Hlus	Kenneth H.	William Fraser, Jr.	William F.
Garry Keller, Jr.	Garry K.	Corey Giese	Larry G.
Carla Lemmer	Werner L.	Jennifer Giese	Greg G.
Craig Mohr	Richard M.	Sherry Goerz	Roger G.
Marc Mohr	David M.	Chantelle Hennig	Harvey H.
Bonnie Nernberg	Kenneth N.	Jesse Luckhardt	Brian L.
Shandra Riedlinger	Mrs. Linda R.	Kristina Roberts	Roger R.
Carolyn Rosher	Mrs. Rosalyn R.	Jamie Scheuerman	Mrs. Sheryl S.
Todd Schultz	Richard S.	Michael Schiemann	Rev. Donald S.
Tammy-Lynn	Larry S.	James Schutz	Robert S.
Lynette Steuber	Eric S.	Amy Swanson	Ken S.
Naomi Stohlmann	Steve S.	Kathy Tomaino	Doran Boume
Joseph Tomaino	Doran Boume	Angela Yaehne	Rod Y.
Michelle Yaehne	Rod Y.		

Adult Class:
Sheila
Webber
Charles Lilly

Adult Class:
Tracy Allen
Edith Carter
Norm Rockney
Denise (Schlecker) William
Doreen Stroh
Kerry Stroh
Gerry Stroh
Marlene Ursel

1990

Tanya Boles	Ivan B.
Shelley	Mrs. Donna B.
Boychuck Tyson	Mrs. Maureen C.
Colban Laine	Randy D.
Davis Angela	Gary G.
Goebel Darla	Mrs. Verna
Kubbernus	Carter Roland L.
Richard	Kenneth N.
Laramee	Rev. William N.
Dwayne	Wayne N.
Nernberg	Stanley S.
Michelle Ney	Rod S.
Jason Nowoczin	Glenn S.
Leanne Schram	KenS.
Geofrey Schutz	Gordon U.
Dwayne	

Sterman Gail
Swanson Curtis
Ussel Bramwell
Denise Dryer
Wanda (nee McKay)
Edmondson
Lynn Hay
Kelly Kerckhof
Doris (nee Albert) Lutz
John Jenkins
Marcel Melanson
Rob Perrin
Wade Rhine
Andrew Rosher
Kristie Williamson

1992

Cody Davis	Randy D.
David Fraser	William F.
Andrea Gabel	Arnold G.
Christel Hennig	DanH.
Shannon Hennig	Darrel H.
Cherie McAllister	Mrs. Eleanor M.
Miranda Mohr	Richard M.
Cindy Nowoczin	Wayne N.
Nicole Propp	Janet P.
Jamie Ray	Elmer R.
Lynette Riedlinger	Mrs. Linda R.
Lana Schutz	RodS.
Christie Smigelski	Larry S.
Shauna Stanley	Mrs. Constance
Charles Swanson	Ken S.
Brandon Swicheniuk	Ray S.
Travis Swicheniuk	Ray S.
Keven Wasylyshyn	Alex W.
Patricia Woodley	Wayne W.

Adult Class:
Rod Hamilton Hali
Hennig Patricia Holt
Craig Letendre David
Osbaldeston Lee
Tinney Tanya Tinney
Trudy Walra ven
Theresa Zukoski

1991

Michelle	Mrs. Marilyn
Blackford	B.
Sarah Burge	Derry B.

Confirmand	Parent's Name
1993	
Sheila Baker Bart	Mrs. Linda B.
Boles Lori Ann	Ivan B.
Bourne Nathan	Doran B.
Burge Kenneth	Derry B.
Hennig John	Harvey H.
Klimochko Laura	Mrs. Judy K.
Maze Amber Miller	Mrs. Robyn M.
Michael Robin	Mrs. Charlotte M.
Amanda	Mrs. Deborah R.
Scheuerman Peter	Mrs. Sheryl S.
Schiemann	Rev. Don S.
Carlene Schultz	Richard S.
Amanda Schutz	Harvey S.
Cody Stroh	Gerry S.

Adult Class: Chris Ambrozic Marie Baron Dianne Petting Morgan Lindmark Rebecca Lindmark Bert Lubbers Christine Minaker Harvey Rankin Marjorie Rankin Tim Starreveld Deanne Thompson Bart van Rootselaar Leigh-Ann van Rootselaar

1994	
Chantelle	Mrs.Marilyn
Blackford Andrew	B.
Gabel	Arnold G.
Wesley Goertz	Roy G.
Kory Hennig Lori	Lyle H.
Knopke Amanda	Fred K.
Pedersen Amanda	Eric P.
Schram Karissa	Stanley S.
Sorenson Carmen	Lester S.
Swicheniuk David	Raymond S.
Ulmer	Randall U.
Vicki Hennig	David H.
Katheryne Polzin	Thomas P.
Jeremy Shepherd	

Adult Class: Linda (Getzinger) Edwards Candas McNab Doreen McNab Lydia McKean-Woodley

Confirmand Parent's Name

Adult - 1956
Jean Unterschultz
Peter Smigelski
Otto Engelhardt

The Adult Group of Confirmands for 1956 above have been added to the list here because they were accidently omitted from the "90th Anniversary Book".

Part Four

Cemetery
... departed saints recognized

St. Matthew Lutheran Church Cemetery

On May 18, 1894, Rev. F. H. Eggers of Great Falls, Montana, met with the original 20 families who later were to become a part of the founding of St. Matthew. The families decided to join the Missouri Synod. The first church service was held with Holy Communion, and according to historical records, St. Matthew Lutheran Cemetery was dedicated on that day.

Over the years the cemetery has been cared for and maintained by the members and has grown to the size it is today. It should always be remembered that this is the last resting place of our brothers and sisters now fallen asleep in Christ. It should also be a reminder for those of us yet living that one day we too shall be called to eternal rest to be forever with the Lord.

Burials within St. Matthew cemetery are open to members of the congregation, Lutheran Church Canada, and members of other congregations which are in altar and pulpit fellowship with us.

Our cemetery recorder, Mr. Otto C. Hennig, has provided us with some very interesting statistics compiled from the records. They are as follows, dated from November 5,1894 to November 5, 1994.

First burial - February 21,1895 - Daniel Gitzel - child - 6 years.
Last burial - October 30,1994 - Elsie M. Kulak - adult - 78 years.

Males-371
Females - 313
Total - 684 burials.
Of the 684 burials, 212 were children 12 years and under. An interesting observation is to be noted in the death rate of the children. The first 50 years (1895-1944) - there were 354 burials. Of the 354,198 were children under the age of 12 years. The last 50 years (1945-1994 there were 330 burials. Of the 330, 14 were children under the age of 12 years.

Years	Total Burials	Males	Females	Children (12 yrs & under)
1895-1899	22	8	14	19
1900-1909	107	57	50	79
1910-1919	99	53	46	47
1920-1929	67	34	33	37
1930-1939	41	22	19	14
1940-1949	37	20	17	5
1950-1959	42	21	21	2
1960-1969	61	42	19	1
1970-1979	80	42	38	7
1980-1989	88	56	32	0
1990-1994	40	16	24	1

Other Statistical Information

1894	no burials		
1923	3	all males	2 children
1944	2	all females	1 child
1957	2	all males	
1965	5	all males	
1982	9	all males	

1940	had the least burials in one year	1 burial
1910	had the most burials in one year	18 burials: 12 were children

Oldest members buried according to records available:
Male: Michael Pall 94 years-buried November 11, 1983
Female: Emelia Wudel 94 years-buried October 21, 1992

Pastors buried in St. Matthew Cemetery
Rev. Henry Mohr   January 17, 1919
Rev. Dr. Emil E. Eberhardt March 29, 1957
Rev. Fred Ulmer   September 7, 1966
Rev. Arthur Gehring   November 29, 1972
Rev. Carl Hennig   August 17, 1987

"Man that is bom of a woman is of few days and full of trouble. He cometh forth like a flower, and is cut down; he fleeth also as a shadow, and continueth not. Behold, Thou hast made my days as an handbreadth; and mine age is as nothing before Thee. Verily, every man at his best state is altogether vanity.

Thus saith the Lord: dust thou art, and unto dust shalt thou return. By one man sin entered into the world and death by sin; and so death passed upon all men, for that all have sinned.

Jesus is the First Fruits of them that sleep, and saith: I am the Resurrection and the Life; he that believeth in Me, though he were dead, yet shall he live; and whosoever liveth and believeth in Me shall never die." *(1)

by Roland Hennig

(1) Reprinted from The Lutheran Agenda, Concordia Publishing House, St Louis, Missouri

"Rest in Peace ·"

A Final Page In A History

After all is said and done and one hundred years completed...

"Finally, the past is history and we shall reflect upon this for lessons to learn from. We shall not forget the great challenges, hardships, moments of glory and victories that were once experienced by our forefathers and relived in our hearts and minds this day as a memorial of their faithfulness to God our Creator.

Although many uncertainties lie before us, we will face our challenges and obstacles with the same courage and faith that our forefathers had. The lessons they taught us, by their Christian example during these preceding one hundred years, can only be measured by the strength of our faith in and loyalty to Christ our Saviour and risen Lord. Just as God was their refuge and sure defense, he will no less be ours today by renewing our commitment to Him. He will never leave us nor forsake us. This is His promise to all His believing people to the end of time. This is our confession. This we believe. Thanks be to God!"

by Roland Hennig

From 1894 - 1994, one hundred years completed, St. Matthew Lutheran Church and
Congregation ... a century of service, commitment and praise.

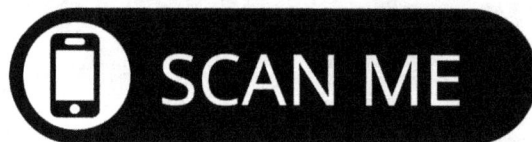

For the newest works by
Reuben A Bauer,
please come to
Readthepast.ca

Thank you for enjoying this book